Pearson Australia
(a division of Pearson Australia Group Pty Ltd)
707 Collins Street, Melbourne, Victoria 3008
PO Box 23360, Melbourne, Victoria 8012
www.pearson.com.au

First published 2014 by Pearson Australia
2017 2016 2015 2014
10 9 8 7 6 5 4 3

Publisher: Kaye De Petro
Project Editor: Aisling Coughlan, Megan Cassar
Editor: Writers Reign, Kirsty Hine
Series Cover Designers: Miranda Costa, Kim Ferguson, Jo Groud and Glen McClay
Designers: Leigh Ashforth, Jay Urbanic and Jeni Burton
Typesetter: Paul Ryan
Copyright & Pictures Editor: Alice McBroom
Cover art: Corbis/Jean-Pierre Lescourret
Illustrators: Xiangyi Mo, Vasja Koman, Bruce Rankin and Guy Holt
Printed and bound in Australia by Pegasus Media & Logistics

ISBN 978 1 4860 1405 7

Pearson Australia Group Pty Ltd ABN 40 004 245 943

Acknowledgements
We would like to thank the following for permission to reproduce copyright material. The following abbreviations are used in this list: t = top, b = bottom, l = left, r = right, c = centre.

Aboriginal Art Online Pty Ltd/Based on information from "Papunya Tula" by Geoffrey Bardon, p. 30r.
Alamy: p. 37; The Art Gallery Collection, p. 59; Richard Ashworth p. 89tr; Peter Barritt, pp. iii, 22b; The Bridgeman Art Library, p. 54; Gianni Dagli Orti, p. 11tr; Dorling Kindersley, p. 17; Les Gibbon, p. 7bl; Paul Glendell, p. 7br; Robert Harding, pp. 89tl, 89cl, 89cr; Robert Preston, p. 92l; Travel Pictures, p. 19l; Hu Weibiao, p. 99; Adam Woolfitt, p. 81.
The British Museum: The Trustees of the British Museum. All rights reserved, pp. 10, 11tl, 11bl, 11br.
Brenda Brown: 'Yuendumu' used by permission of Warlayirti Artists, p. 30l.
Corbis: Charles Lenars, p. 22t; Keren Su, p. 92r; Penny Tweedie, p. 28; Roger Wood, pp. 89bl, 89br.
Dreamstime: pp. 19r, 21.
Getty Images: pp. 24b, 39; Dave Einsel, p. 24t; Getty/Farrell Grehan, cover, p. i.
Science Photo Library: Sheila Terry, pp. 46, 67.
Adrian Shepherd: p. 86.
Charles Tait: pp. 7 tl, 7tr.
Thinkstock: pp. 1, 33, 49, 65, 95.

Every effort has been made to trace and acknowledge copyright. However, if any infringement has occurred, the publishers tender their apologies and invite the copyright holders to contact them.

Some of the images used in *Pearson History New South Wales Activity Book* 7 might have associations with deceased Indigenous Australians. Please be aware that these images might cause sadness or distress in Aboriginal or Torres Strait Islander communities.

CONTENTS

Overview of the ancient world

Chapter 1: Overview of the ancient world 1

1.1 In the beginning ... 1
1.2 Map of Human Migration 3
1.3 Technological triumphs 4
1.4 New or old? 5
1.5 Primary sources: Skara Brae 7
1.6 Timeline of Sumer 9
1.7 Primary sources: The Nabonidus cylinder, Sumer 10
1.8 Primary sources: The Royal Tombs of Ur, Sumer 11
1.9 Sumer: the land between the rivers 13
1.10 A typical Sumerian settlement 15

Depth study 1: Investigating the ancient past

Chapter 2: Investigating the Ancient Past 17

2.1 Timelines 17
2.2 Historical information: where does it come from? 19
2.3 Historical information: how is it interpreted? 21
2.4 Working like a historian 23
2.5 Timeline and maps of ancient Australia 25
2.6 Primary sources: Ancient Australia 27
2.7 The Rainbow Serpent: Ancient Australia 29
2.8 Circles and lines: Ancient Australia 30
2.9 Torres Strait Islanders: Ancient Australia 31

Depth study 2: The Mediterranean world

Chapter 3: Ancient Egypt 33

3.1 Timeline of Ancient Egypt 33
3.2 Write like an Egyptian 34
3.3 Map of Ancient Egypt 35
3.4 Primary sources: the apprentice scribe 37
3.5 Primary sources: The Nubian Slaves 39
3.6 Reconstruct the pyramid 40
3.7 Rich or poor? 41
3.8 Regalia and power 43
3.9 The Gods 45
3.10 The rhythm of life 47
3.11 Making mummies 48

Chapter 4: Ancient Greece 49

4.1 Timeline of Ancient Greece 49
4.2 True or false? 50
4.3 The geography of Ancient Greece 51
4.4 Primary sources 53
4.5 The Persian Wars 55
4.6 Spartans and Athenians 57
4.7 Generations of Gods 59
4.8 Oracles and prophecies 61
4.9 It's all Greek to me! 63

Chapter 5: Ancient Rome 65

5.1 Location of Ancient Rome 65
5.2 Timeline of Ancient Rome 66
5.3 Looking at a primary source 67
5.4 Roman Gods 68
5.5 Looking at a primary document 69
5.6 Numbers and alphabet of Ancient Rome 71
5.7 Spiral word puzzle 72
5.8 People of Ancient Rome 73
5.9 Roman Warfare 75
5.10 Famous Romans 77
5.11 Legacies of Ancient Rome 79

Depth study 3: The Asian world

Chapter 6: Ancient India 81

6.1 Timeline of Ancient India 81
6.2 Map of Ancient India 82
6.3 An epic cartoon 83
6.4 Primary Sources 85
6.5 Volumes of Vedas 87
6.6 A place in the world 88
6.7 Primary sources: The Indus Valley 89
6.8 The Ajunta Caves 91
6.9 Buddha: riches to rags 93

Chapter 7: Ancient China 95

7.1 Timeline of Ancient China 95
7.2 The Early Dynasties 96
7.3 Map of Ancient China 97
7.4 Primary sources 99
7.5 Chinese philosophies 101
7.6 Climb the Great Wall of China 103
7.7 The odd one out 104
7.8 Who am I? 105
7.9 Word search 107

HOW TO USE THE PEARSON HISTORY NEW SOUTH WALES ACTIVITY BOOK 7

The *Pearson History New South Wales Activity Book 7* has been designed to further consolidate students' historical concepts and historical skills in accordance with the New South Wales Board of Studies syllabus for the Australian Curriculum: History.

The Activity Book consists of seven chapters. Each chapter incorporates a range of the following features, which have been constructed to engage students in a variety of learning styles to strengthen their skills.

MAP WORK AND TIMELINE ACTIVITIES:

- Build students' understanding of the importance of location and geography in history.
- Enable students to identify patterns of movement and change within societies.
- Further develop students' understanding of chronology.

EVIDENCE-BASED ACTIVITIES AND QUESTIONS:

- Employ a variety of sources for students to examine critically:
  - primary sources
  - secondary sources
  - written sources
  - visual sources.

LITERACY-BASED ACTIVITIES AND QUESTIONS:

- Are designed to test and consolidate students' knowledge of key historical words and phrases.
- Include:
  - stories from the past
  - creation stories, stories about gods or traditional stories from primary sources
  - crosswords
  - word finds
  - matching words and definitions.

CHAPTER 1 OVERVIEW: THE ANCIENT WORLD

1.1 IN THE BEGINNING ...

Big bang — 4.5 billion years ago Earth was formed

3000 million years · 600 million years · 500 million years · 400 million years · 300 million years · 200 million years · 100 million years · Today

First cells
Oldest rocks
Shells
Land plants
Earliest fish
Fish
Reptiles
Early plants
Primitive mammals
Dinosaurs
Flowering plants
Modern mammals
Trees
Apes
Homo sapiens appears (120 000 BC)

Pre-Cambrian era · Palaeozoic era · Mesozoic era · Cenozoic era

SOURCE 1.1.1 Timeline of the Earth's development

1 Look carefully at the timeline dating from the Big Bang to today (Source 1.1.1) and answer the following questions.

a Approximately how many years after the Earth was formed did *Homo sapiens* first appear?

____

____

b Name two living things that predate *Homo sapiens.*

____

____

2 Look carefully at the timeline dating from 75 000 BC to today (Source 1.1.1) and complete the following tasks.

a Add the following events to the timeline by placing a coloured dot in the correct location to represent:

- 38 500 BC, when goats and sheep were domesticated in Sumer (red dot)
- 45 000 BC, when rice growing started in China (green dot)
- 53 500 BC, when the wheel and plough were invented (blue dot).

b Research the Stone Age on the internet or in your school library. Use your findings to show the periods of Old Stone Age (Palaeolithic) and New Stone Age (Neolithic) on Source 1.1.2.

c Indicate whether the following statements are true or false.

	TRUE OR FALSE?
The last Ice Age occurred in 38 000BC.	
By 45 000BC humans had settled in Australia.	
Southern Asia was settled before South America.	
The eruption of Toba in Indonesia occurred before Asia was settled.	

75 000 BC Human migration reaches southern Asia

70 000 BC Eruption of Toba, Indonesia

50 000 BC Humans settle Australia

38 000 BC Humans settle Europe

16 000–10 000 BC Last Ice Age

15 000 BC European Stone Age paintings

10 000 BC Humans reach South America

5500 BC Irrigation in Sumer

75 000 BC 60 000 BC 45 000 BC 30 000 BC 15 000 BC Today

7000 BC Chinese pottery

2400 BC Stonehenge built

SOURCE 1.1.2 Timeline of human development

3 Read the metaphor below. A metaphor is a figure of speech that expresses an idea through the image of another object.

In the first 25 years of the 45-year-old man's life, the Earth was formed and oxygen became common in the atmosphere. In the last six months of his life, fish appeared then plants and reptiles. In the last three months dinosaurs appeared and disappeared, primitive mammals roamed the Earth and flowering plants grew. In the last week of his life, modern mammals and trees spread across the Earth. In the last few days, our ancestors, *Homo sapiens* appeared. When the man just closed his eyes to blink, the Old and New Stone Ages came and went. When he opened his eyes again, it was TODAY!

a What is the 45-year-old man being used to explain?

____

____

____

b Does the metaphor help your understanding? Why or why not?

____

____

____

1.2 MAP OF HUMAN MIGRATION

Look carefully at the map and timeline to complete the following tasks.

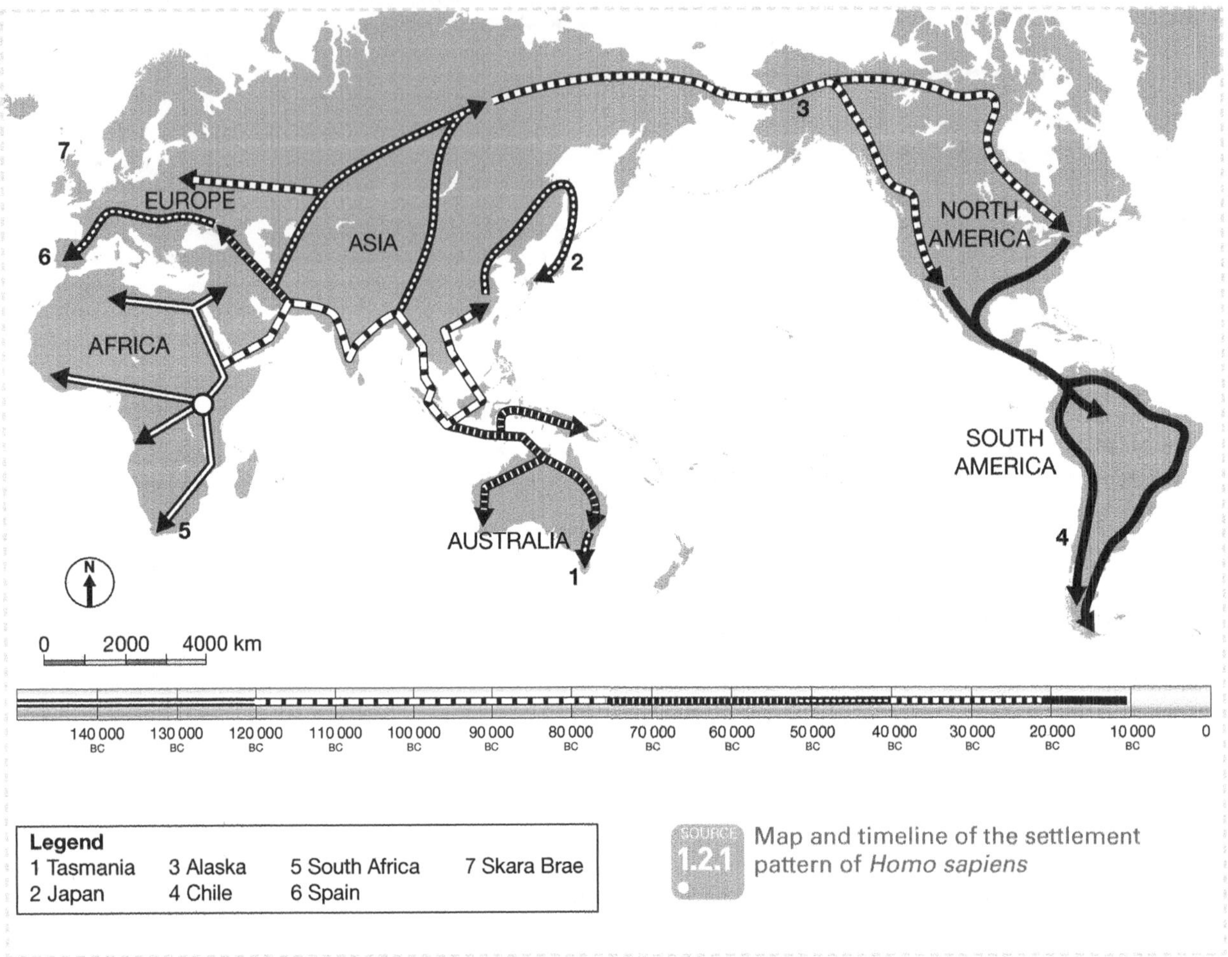

SOURCE 1.2.1 Map and timeline of the settlement pattern of *Homo sapiens*

1 a List the continents settled by *Homo sapiens* in chronological order of settlement. Start with the continent of origin.

___

b Refer to your list and explain why you think this pattern of migration occurred.

___

___

2 Indicate whether the following statements about *Homo sapiens*'s migration are true or false.

	TRUE OR FALSE?
Homo sapiens who migrated to Alaska came from Chile.	
Japan was settled at about the same time as Tasmania.	
Australia was settled between 120 000BC and 100 000BC.	
Homo sapiens reached Southern Asia before settling in Europe.	
Most of North America was settled by 20 000BC.	
Nothern and Southern Europe were settled by 50 000BC.	

1.3 TECHNOLOGICAL TRIUMPHS

Early humans were very resourceful. They invented items that improved their lifestyle and increased their chances of survival. These advances may seem of little importance to us in our technological world; however, to Stone Age humans, their inventions were incredibly useful and they sparked a technological revolution.

Look at the illustrations of Stone Age inventions and answer the following questions. Conduct research on the internet or in your school library to help you find the answers.

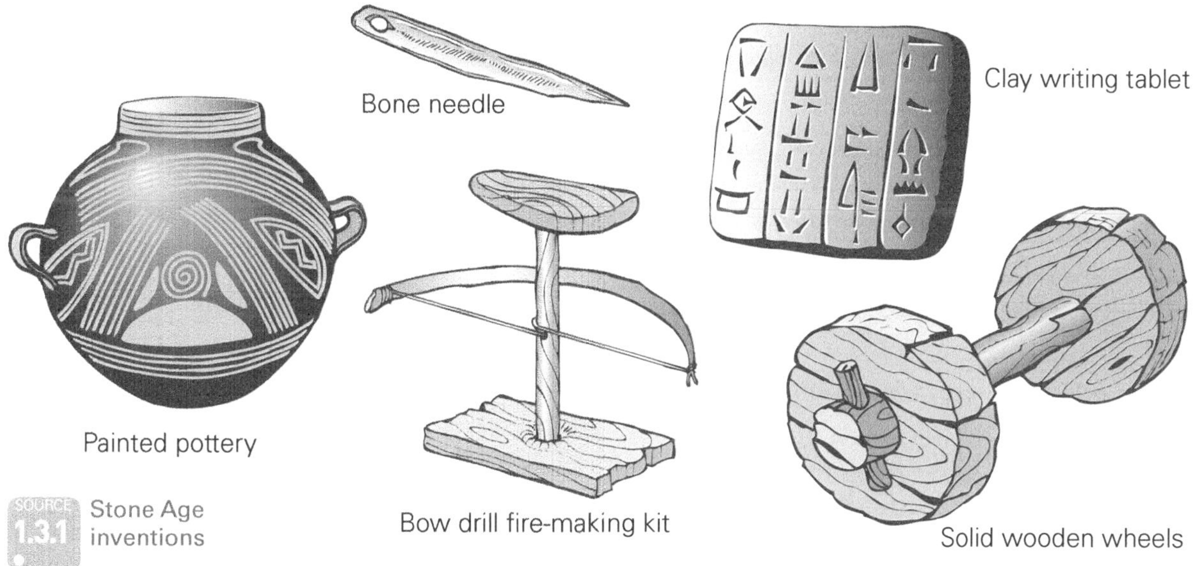

SOURCE 1.3.1 Stone Age inventions

1 a What is the chronological order of these inventions? Write the name of the invention in the correct place on the table below.

b Next to the name of each invention explain how the invention improved the lives of people of the Stone Age.

INVENTION ORDER	NAME OF INVENTION	THE IMPROVEMENT RESULTING FROM THE INVENTION
1st (oldest)		
2nd		
3rd		
4th		
5th (most recent)		

2 Describe the raw materials that would have been used to produce these inventions and explain why these particular resources were used.

____

____

____

____

NEW OR OLD?

1 Below is a jumbled list of phrases that relate to the Old and New Stone Ages. Identify and highlight all the phrases that relate to the Old Stone Age. Use a different colour to highlight all the words and phrases that relate to the New Stone Age. Conduct research on the internet or in your school library to help you find the answers.

All the men hunted small and large animals	Dates to a time before 10 000 BC
Permanent settlements were established	Jericho was built at this time
Farmers and herders	Nomadic lifestyle
Foods were stored for future use	Animals were tamed and provided meat, skins and milk
The Sahara was green grassland	Very few people in a region
Wild grass seeds were sown as crops	Women and children gathered fruit, nuts and honey
Population concentrated in one area	A varied diet
Trade developed	Religious beliefs developed

2 Look at the two drawings below and decide which drawing is a typical Palaeolithic scene and which is a Neolithic scene. Show your answer by clearly labelling each drawing.

3 Explain the reasons for your decision in the previous question.

4 Write a paragraph describing four differences between life in Palaeolithic times and life in Neolithic times.

5 Historians use some odd-sounding terms, such as 'Palaeolithic' and 'Neolithic'. Where do they come from? Look up the meanings of 'neo', 'palaeo' and 'lithic', using an English dictionary.

a From what language do these terms originate?

b What does each term mean?

PRIMARY SOURCES: SKARA BRAE

Skara Brae is located on the Orkney Islands, Scotland. It is Europe's most complete Neolithic village. In 1999, it was given World Heritage status. Skara Brae was first exposed in 1850 when a storm blew away a lot of the overlying sand dunes. It was further exposed after another storm in 1924. Radiocarbon dating indicates that Skara Brae was inhabited between 3200 BC and 2200 BC. Parts of the village are still buried.

SOURCE 1.5.1 Aerial photo of Skara Brae

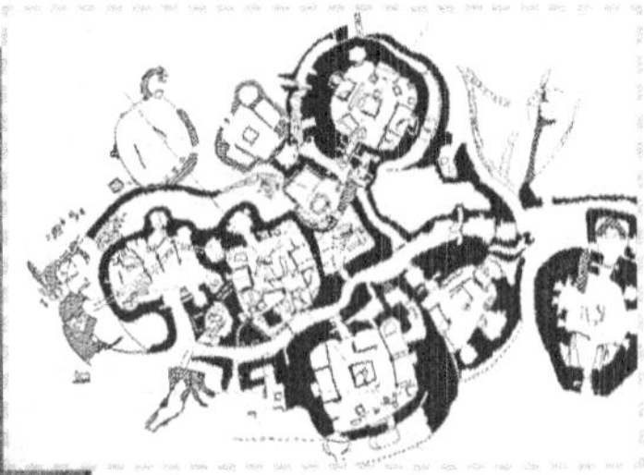

Houses
Workshop
The only building with its own entrance
Evidence of tool making
Coast
Houses
Only entrance to village

SOURCE 1.5.2 Layout of Skara Brae

SOURCE 1.5.3 Low, narrow stone alleyways linking the houses

- The village was built into a large Palaeolithic rubbish heap called a midden. It contained the remains of cattle, sheep, fish and shellfish, and egg shells of sea birds. There were also seeds and remains of wheat and barley.
- The midden insulated the village from the cold, harsh winter climate.

SOURCE 1.5.4 Wide view of a typical house

Large box beds made of stone slabs
Cupboard
Open fireplace
Dresser with shelves
Narrow doorway to enter the house, bolted from inside. The door was a slab of stone
Limpet tank filled with water, possibly the household water supply
Small box beds made of stone slabs and supports

- There were eight buildings in the village. They were connected by a series of narrow passages. At its largest, the village had 50 to 100 inhabitants.
- Houses were all of the same basic design. There was a large, spacious square room. The average house size was 40 square metres.
- Each house had a central fire place. There were beams made of whale bone or driftwood to support the roof. The roof was a thick layer of turf, animal skins, seaweed or straw.
- The houses had a drainage system and a primitive toilet.
- Many tools and artefacts were found at the site—needles, knives, adzes, shovels, small bowls, rope made of twisted leather and pottery.

The three basic and essential requirements for survival are food, shelter and safety. Look at all the information very closely. Using evidence from these sources, explain how the inhabitants of Skara Brae met their basic requirements. Find three examples each of food, shelter and safety. Then write a paragraph for each requirement, using these examples.

SOURCE 1.5.5 Reconstruction of a typical house

The inhabitants of Skara Brae met their basic need for food by ...

____

____

____

____

____

____

____

The inhabitants of Skara Brae met their basic need for safety by ...

____

____

____

____

____

The inhabitants of Skara Brae met their basic need for shelter by ...

____

____

____

____

____

____

1.6 TIMELINE OF SUMER

7000 BC

7000 Evidence of metalwork—copper, silver, gold, lead

6000 BC

6000 Evidence of pottery objects. The flood?

5000 BC

4000 BC

4000 Weaving of textiles on a large scale—wool, linen, palm fibre

3400 Growth of cities across Mesopotamia

3150 Records kept using picture writing (pictographs)

3000 BC

2800 Gilgamesh is ruler

2550 Royal tombs of Ur

2450 Wedge-shaped cuneiform writing used

2300 King Sargon of Akkad unites Sumer

2100 Ur becomes the new capital; Akkad Empire collapses

2000 BC

1800 Hammurabi unites Mesopotamia

1600 Hittites from central Turkey raid Sumer. End of Sumerian civilisation

1000 BC

SOURCE 1.6.1 Timeline of Sumer

1 The timeline shows some important events in the history of the Sumerian civilisation. After looking at the timeline carefully, indicate whether the following statements about Sumer are true or false.

	TRUE OR FALSE?
The Sumerians wove fabrics of linen and wool.	
Pottery was not made until 4000 BC.	
There was a growth of cities about 3000 BC.	
Ur became the capital city of Sumer in about 2100 BC.	
There is evidence that Sumerians worked with metals in 9000 BC.	
Cuneiform writing was used before pictograph writing.	
Hammurabi, Gilgamesh and Sargon were all rulers.	
The Akkadian people ruled Sumer between 2300 BC and 2100 BC.	
The Hittites were a particular group of people in Sumer.	
The height of the Sumerian civilisation was from 3500 BC to 1600 BC.	
Pictograph writing uses wedge-shaped symbols.	
Gilgamesh was a ruler at a time before Sargon ruled.	

2 The Sumerian civilisation was considered very advanced for its time. Provide at least two pieces of evidence from the timeline that demonstrate Sumer's superior human and social organisation.

___

___

___

PRIMARY SOURCES: THE NABONIDUS CYLINDER, SUMER

The Nabonidus cylinder was one of four cylinders found by Leonard Woolley in the ziggurat of Ur, in Sumer. Each cylinder was located in a corner of the temple. The cylinders were associated with the Babylonian King Nabonidus, who ruled between 555 BC and 539 BC.

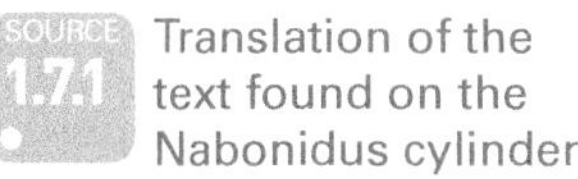

SOURCE 1.7.1 Translation of the text found on the Nabonidus cylinder

> I am Nabonidus, king of Babylon … devotee of the great gods … which Ur-Nammu, a former king, built it but did not finish it, his son Shulgi finished its building …
>
> Now that ziggurat had become old, and I undertook the construction of that ziggurat on the foundations … following the original plan with bitumen and baked brick. I rebuilt it for Sin, the lord of the gods of heaven and underworld, the god of gods, who lives in the great heavens …
>
> Sin, lord of the gods, king of the gods of heaven and underworld, god of gods, who lives in the great heavens, when you enter with joy into this temple may the welfare of … the temple of the great divinity, be always on your lips. And let the fear of your great divinity; be in the heart of the people so that they will not sin against your great divinity.

Carefully read the extract of the inscription of the Nabonidus cylinder. Then answer the following questions.

1 Which leader originally had the temple built in Ur?

____

2 Approximately when do you think this cylinder would have been made? Explain how you decided on this date.

____

____

____

SOURCE 1.7.2 Carving of Nabonidus, 555–539 BC, now at the British Museum

3 Give two reasons why Nabonidus decided to have construction completed on the ziggurat.

____

____

____

4 Why do you think four cylinders with these types of inscriptions were placed in the four corners of the temple?

____

____

____

1.8 PRIMARY SOURCES: THE ROYAL TOMBS OF UR, SUMER

Evidence of the Sumerian civilisation lay buried under sand for thousands of years. Over the last 200 years, the history of Sumer has been gradually revealed, as archaeologists have conducted digs to unearth artefacts. Leonard Woolley was the director of excavations around the ancient city of Ur and made many discoveries, including ancient tombs. Of these, sixteen had valuable objects in them, so were named the Royal Tombs. At one end of the burial pit, a chamber was located with the skeleton and belongings of a woman called Pu-abi.

1 Items located near Pu-abi's head and shoulders include a cylinder seal, with cuneiform writing saying 'Lady Pu-abi'.

The jewellery of Pu-abi. The upper part of her body was covered in multi-coloured beads of gold, silver, lapis lazuli and cornelian, as were her headdress and necklace. From Grave 800, the Royal Cemetery of Ur, southern Iraq, about 2600 BC, now at the British Museum

2 Dagger with intricate gold sheath, second half of third millennium BC, from Royal Tomb at Ur, now at Archaeological Museum Baghdad

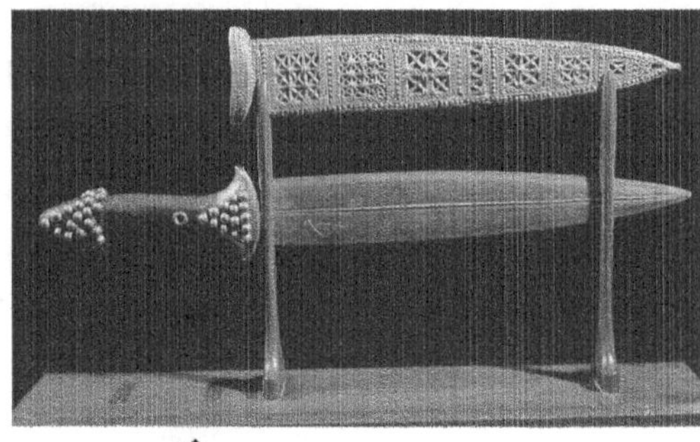

3 The remains of a sledge and wood chest were found in the death pit. Also found were the bodies of two oxen, their groomsmen, five armed men and fifteen attendants. Twelve of the attendants were women who wore simpler versions of Queen Pu-abi's headdress.

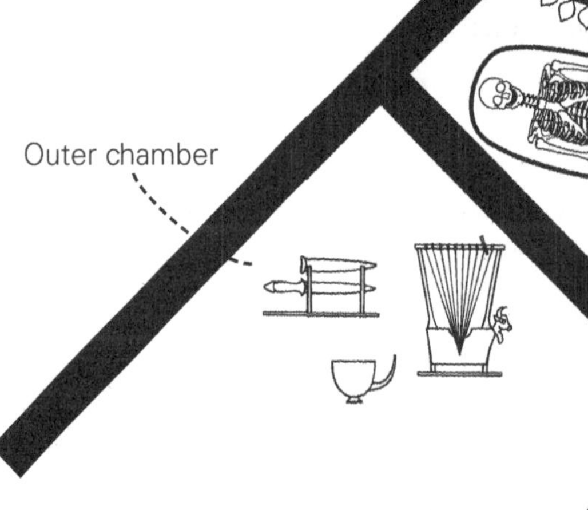

SOURCE 1.8.1 The burial chamber of Pu-abi

4 Gold fluted bowl with spout, now at the British Museum

5 The lyre, a wooden musical instrument. From Ur, c. 2600 BC, now at the British Museum

Look carefully at all the evidence in the burial chamber of Pu-abi and complete the following questions.

1 Outline three pieces of evidence that shows the person buried in the chamber was important in Sumerian society.

2 What do you think was the purpose of the sledge that was found in the tomb?

3 What materials were used to make Pu-abi's jewellery?

4 List all the materials that were used to make the artefacts in the Royal Tombs.

5 Why do you think that items such as a musical instrument, a dagger and a sledge were put in the tomb?

6 Complete a Venn diagram to show the similarities and differences between the discoveries in the inner chamber and those in the outer chamber.

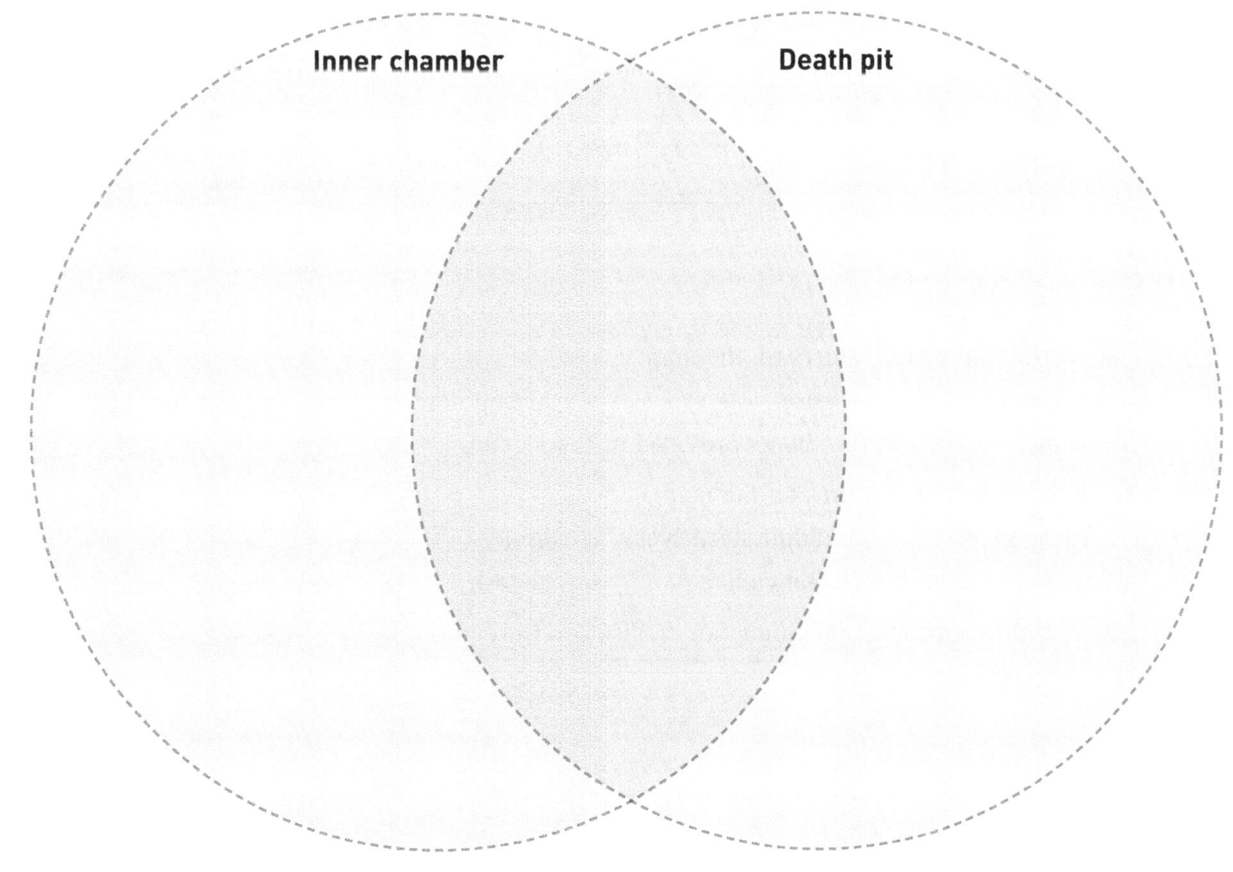

1.9 SUMER: THE LAND BETWEEN THE RIVERS

Mesopotamia is the name given to the land between the Tigris and Euphrates rivers. The land occupied by the Sumerians was the south-eastern part of this area.

Look carefully at the map and conduct research on the internet or in your school library to help you complete the following tasks.

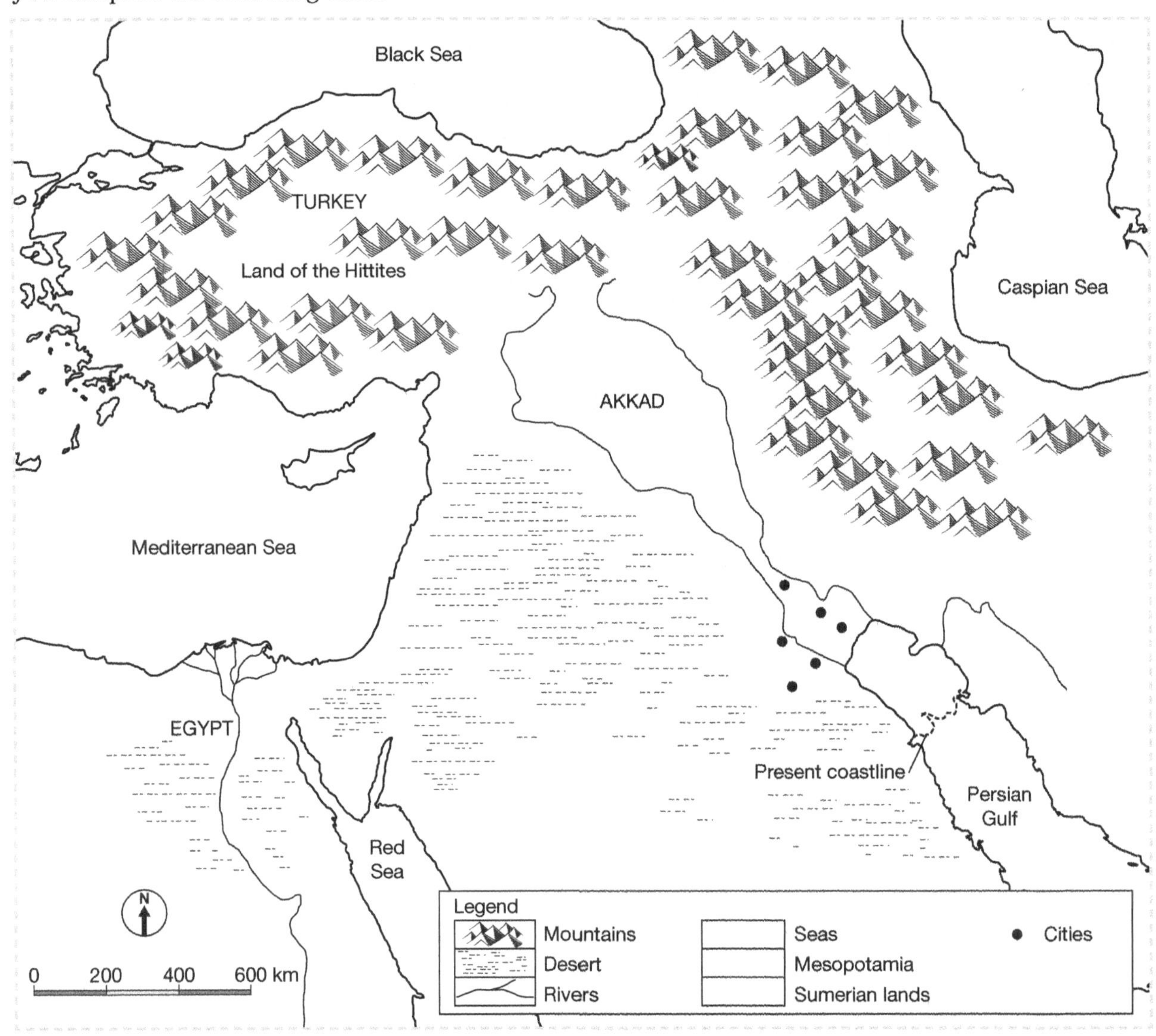

SOURCE 1.9.1 Sumer lands and surrounding areas

1 Colour the following features on the map:

- rivers
- seas
- Mesopotamia
- Sumerian lands.

Show these colours in the spaces provided in the legend.

2 Label the following features on the map:

- Tigris River
- Euphrates River
- Eridu
- Ur
- Uruk
- Babylon
- Lagash
- Nippur.

3 Describe the location of the Sumerian civilisation in relation to the neighbouring civilisations.

____

____

____

4 Rank the four ancient civilisations shown on the map from largest to smallest in size.

5 Compare the geography of the four civilisations. With which civilisation/s does Sumer have the most in common? Explain.

6 Explain why Sumerian settlements did not expand to the east and west of Babylon.

7 Give two reasons why Mesopotamia was an attractive location for settlements such as those of the Sumerian and Akkadian people.

8 About 5000 years ago, Sumerian cities were in a different position in relation to the coastline than they are today. The map shows the coastline changes. Describe how the coastline has changed and suggest a reason why this has happened.

9 The Hittites caused the eventual decline of Sumer. Where was the homeland of the Hittites?

1.10 A TYPICAL SUMERIAN SETTLEMENT

Look at the illustration above of some of the occupations of Sumerians in a typical settlement.

1. Find each of the numbered occupations (1–12) in the illustration.
2. Using the table opposite, describe each occupation and explain why each activity was important for the survival of the settlement. Conduct research on the internet or in your school library for information.

OCCUPATION	DESCRIPTION OF OCCUPATION	IMPORTANCE OF OCCUPATION FOR SURVIVAL
1		
2		
3		
4		
5		
6		
7		
8		
9		
10		
11		
12		

CHAPTER 2: INVESTIGATING THE ANCIENT PAST

2.1 TIMELINES

'History' is a Greek word that means 'the investigation and study of past human events'. Historians reconstruct events from the past through the objective examination of documents and artefacts. Historians also use timelines to sort and visually display past events in chronological order. Historical timelines can cover any period from the start of civilisation to the present day.

> A nation which does not know what it was yesterday, does not know what it is today, nor what it is trying to do.
>
> US President and Nobel Prize winner, Woodrow Wilson (1856–1924)

1 What do you understand the study of history to be about?

____

____

____

____

2 Explain why US President Woodrow Wilson considered history to be important.

____

____

____

____

3 Complete the following tasks. Conduct research on the internet or in your school library to help you.

a What do 'BC' and 'AD' mean?

____

____

b What do 'BCE' and 'CE' mean?

____

____

c Explain why historians sometimes choose to use 'BCE' and 'CE' for dating events rather than 'BC' and 'AD'.

4 a Read the following model timeline of the Roman civilisation and the annotations.

3000 BC

③ 800 BC

753 BC Romulus kills Remus and founds Rome — Roman monarchy

509 BC Romans defeat Etruscans

400 BC

Roman Empire

44 BC Julius Caesar assassinated

1 AD

Roman Empire ①

400 AD ④

476 AD Last Roman emperor deposed ②

① Eras are shown on the timeline. Eras are times during which similar conditions or rulers existed.

② Key dates and events

③ A broken timeline means that some years have been skipped or left out. Remember to keep the same scale for the whole timeline.

④ From the year 1AD, the AD dates increase, moving to the bottom. From the year 1CE, the BC dates increase, moving towards the top.

Ancient Rome timeline

b Now draw your own timeline of the Maya people of Central America. Draw it in the space provided above. The key historical events are shown below.

- Pre-classical period 2000 BC –250 AD
- Classical period 250–800 AD
- Post-classical period 800–1500 AD
- First Maya settlement 1800 BC
- First Maya writing 250 BC
- Peak of Maya civilisation 700 AD
- Spanish conquerors invade Maya lands 1500 AD

2.2 HISTORICAL INFORMATION: WHERE DOES IT COME FROM?

Historical evidence is all around us. Wherever people live they leave evidence of their lifestyles, culture and beliefs. Your house, street and suburb may be evidence that future generations investigate to learn about our world, just as we study places such as Pompeii to learn about Ancient Rome.

Sources of historical evidence can be many and varied, as shown below.

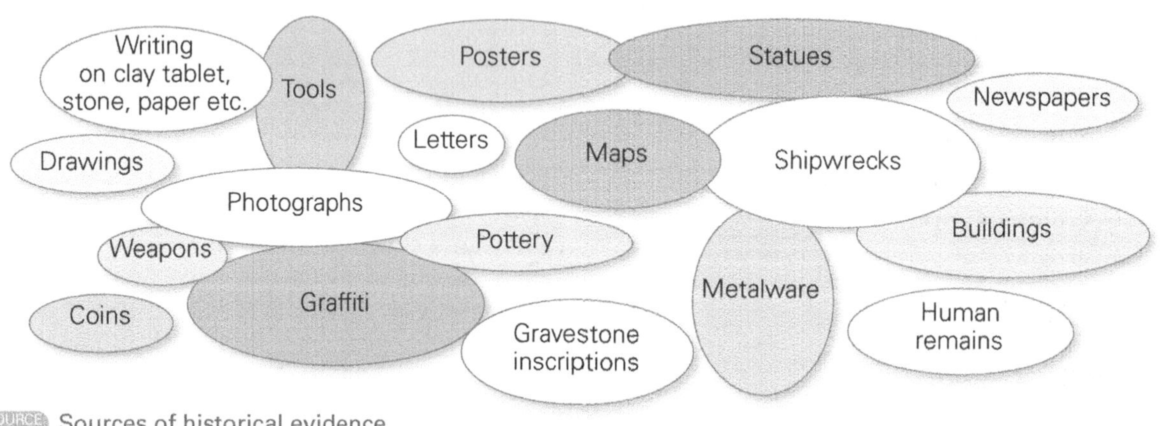

SOURCE 2.2.1 Sources of historical evidence

Historical sources may be classified as either primary or secondary sources. Conduct some research on the internet or in your school library on the differences between primary and secondary sources.

1 Look at the list of sources below and classify them as either primary (by circling in red) or secondary (by circling in blue).

- something created after an event
- first-hand information of an event
- *Pearson History New South Wales Student Book 7*
- something created at the time of an event
- an eyewitness report
- the movie *Gladiator*
- a reconstruction of an event
- the Egyptian pyramids

2 Look at the following sources. For each source state if it is primary or secondary and explain why you decided on this classification.

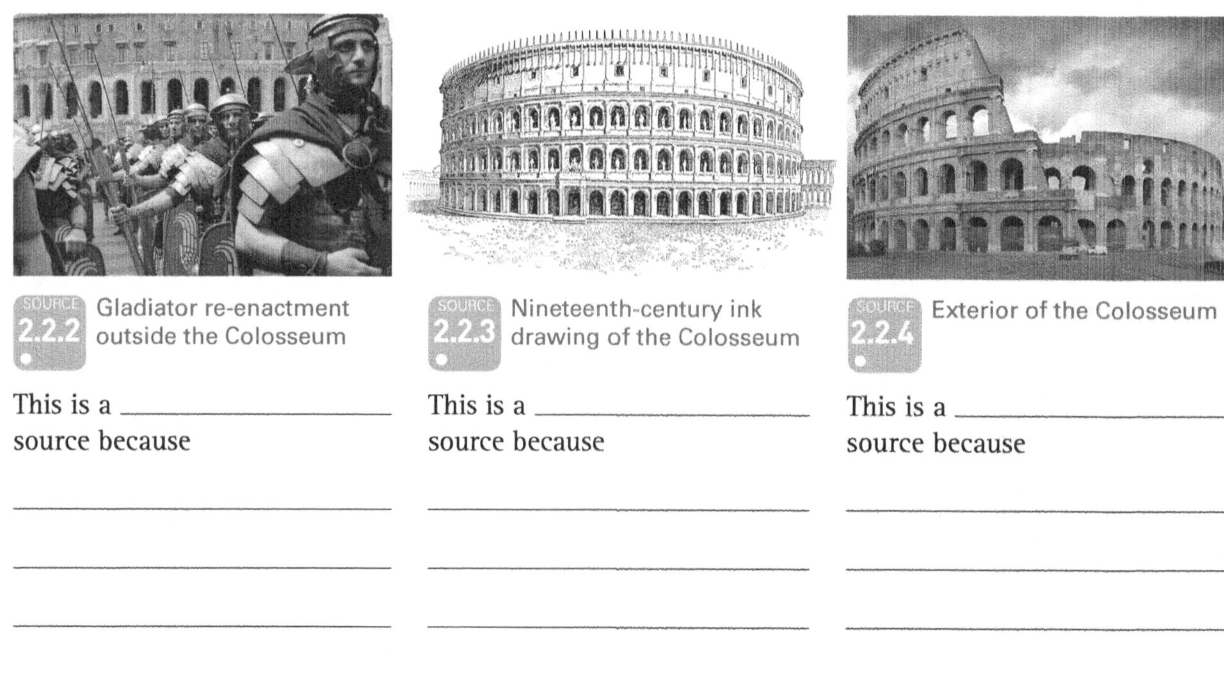

SOURCE 2.2.2 Gladiator re-enactment outside the Colosseum

SOURCE 2.2.3 Nineteenth-century ink drawing of the Colosseum

SOURCE 2.2.4 Exterior of the Colosseum

This is a ______________ source because

____

____

____

____

This is a ______________ source because

____

____

____

____

This is a ______________ source because

____

____

____

____

3 Historians work with other professionals to construct accounts of the past. These experts include archaeologists, anthropologists, etymologists, linguists and conservators. Research what each of these experts does, on the internet or in your school library. Which expert would the historian consult to obtain the following?

a a translation of an Ancient Roman diary written in Latin

____

b a dating of arrowheads and flints found at a Stone Age site

____

c a translation of Maya picture writing

____

d an explanation of how Ancient Greek pottery was unearthed in India

____

e access to valuable and preserved historical documents in a museum

____

f an explanation of the influence of Ancient Greek words in the English language

____

4 Explain which of the following would be the better source to use for historical information:

a information obtained from an internet blog about Christopher Columbus and his voyages *or* a museum display of artefacts from Columbus's ship

____

____

____

b letters written by philosophers living in Ancient Greece or a book about Greek philosophy written in 2010 AD.

____

____

____

5 You are researching the Stone Age. Refer to Source 2.2.1 and list three types of historical evidence you would not choose to investigate. Explain why you made your choice.

____

____

____

____

____

____

____

____

HISTORICAL INFORMATION: HOW IS IT INTERPRETED?

Collecting historical sources is an important part of finding out about the past. Analysing and interpreting the sources is another important part of the process of putting the pieces of the historical jigsaw together.

Historical sources can be sorted into 'fact' and 'opinion' sources. Both primary and secondary sources should be analysed to assess if they are proven facts or if they are merely guesses at what might have happened based on too little evidence or a point of view.

1 Analyse the historical sources below to decide whether they are fact or opinion. Give a reason for each answer.

... Great are the Emperor's achievements ...
All people under heaven
Work with a common purpose.
Tools and measures are the same ...
The written script is made the same ...
He defines the laws leaving no one in doubt,
Making known what is forbidden ...
No evil is tolerated,
So all strive to be excellent people ...
None dare to be lazy ...
The ordinary people know peace ...
People help each other,
There are no robbers or thieves:
People delight in his rule ...
Wherever life is found,
All acknowledge his supreme rule ....

SOURCE 2.3.1 From a 219 BC inscription ordered by Emperor Shi Huangdi (Qin dynasty, 221–206 BC) and written by Li Ssu, his prime minister

SOURCE 2.3.2 A terracotta general of the Qin dynasty (221–206 BC), Ancient China

This source is ______________________
because

____

____

____

____

____

This source is ______________________
because

____

____

____

____

____

2 Interpreting a historical source can involve finding out:

- *who* created it (the civilisation)
- *what* it is and shows about the past (the culture, beliefs, lifestyle)
- *where* it was created (the location)
- *when* it was created (the date)
- *why* it was created (the function or purpose).

Look carefully at the sources below and interpret each one—find out *who, what, where, when, why*.

SOURCE 2.3.3 Part of a thirteenth-century BC painting depicting an agricultural scene, from the Tomb of Sennedjem in Dehr al-Madinah, Egypt

Who ______________________________

What ______________________________

Where ______________________________

When ______________________________

Why ______________________________

SOURCE 2.3.4 Ancient Sumer gold and lapis lazuli plaque showing war scene, 2500 BC. Found in the Royal Tombs of Ur.

Who ______________________________

What ______________________________

Where ______________________________

When ______________________________

Why ______________________________

WORKING LIKE A HISTORIAN

In order to build up a picture of the past, historians collect, assess and interpret sources, develop an idea about what happened in the past (a hypothesis), continue to collect evidence, keep checking that the idea is still accurate and alter the original idea if new, different evidence emerges.

1 Look at the following diagram, which visually explains how historians work. Look also at how historians used this model to piece together the history of our hominid ancestor, 3.2 million-year-old 'Lucy'.

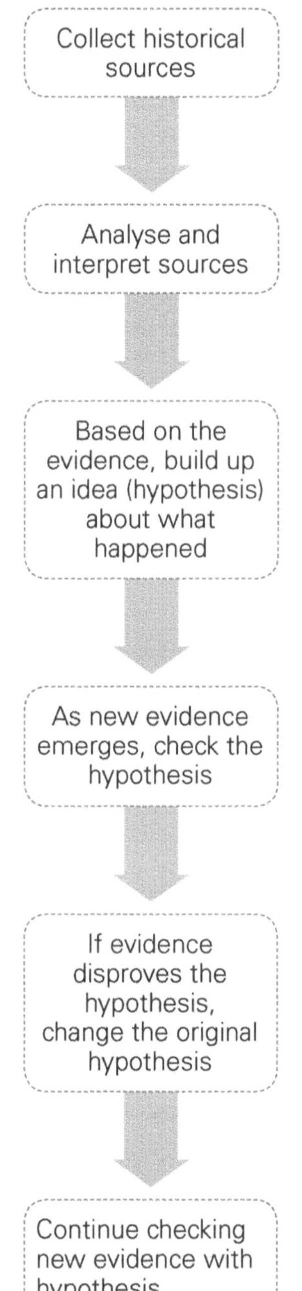

Collect sources

- 1974 field trip
- Hadar, Ethiopia, Africa
- 40 per cent of skeleton found
- Small skull capacity
- Walked on two legs
- Recognised as very old hominid ancestor to humans

First evidence

- Radiocarbon dating
- Stratigraphy dating
- Comparison with other hominid skeletons
- Dated at 3.2 million years old
- Skeleton named 'Lucy'

Hypothesis 1

- Oldest hominid skeleton ever found
- Controversy about whether skeleton is a new species but not enough evidence

Later evidence

- 1978 archaeological dig
- Ancient hominid footprints found in volcanic ash
- Laetoli, Tanzania, Africa
- Three more skeletons like Lucy found
- Other skeletons same age as Lucy

Hypothesis 2

- Confirmed new species of hominid called *Australopithecus afarensis*

- Fieldworkers are collecting new evidence for interpretation and analysis

2 Practise working like a historian by completing the following steps on the incomplete flow chart opposite.

- Look at the flow chart.
- Assess and interpret the evidence.
- Develop an idea about what you think happened and explain why you think this is what happened.
- Write your answer in the space labelled 'Hypothesis 1' on the flow chart.

3 Now look at the new historical evidence labelled 'Later evidence' on the flow chart. Review this evidence, keeping in mind your hypothesis. Does your original hypothesis need changing? Write and explain your hypothesis in the space labelled 'Hypothesis 2' on the flow chart.

Collect sources

- Accidental discovery by two hikers
- Found September, 1991
- Glacier between Italy and Austria in Otztal Alps
- Corpse retrieved for identification
- Items around corpse collected and taken with corpse to mortuary

First evidence

- Corpse in glacier
- Upper body exposed as ice melted
- Common for victims of mountaineering to die, be buried in snow and be discovered when ice melts
- Corpse had experienced a blow to the back of head

Hypothesis 1

Later evidence

- Clothes of corpse included goat, bear and deer skin coat, loin cloth, leggings, cap
- The coat and shoes were made of grass matting
- Belongings included flint tools, bow and arrows, copper axe and dagger
- Corpse carbon dating showed age at between 3350 BC and 3100 BC

Hypothesis 2

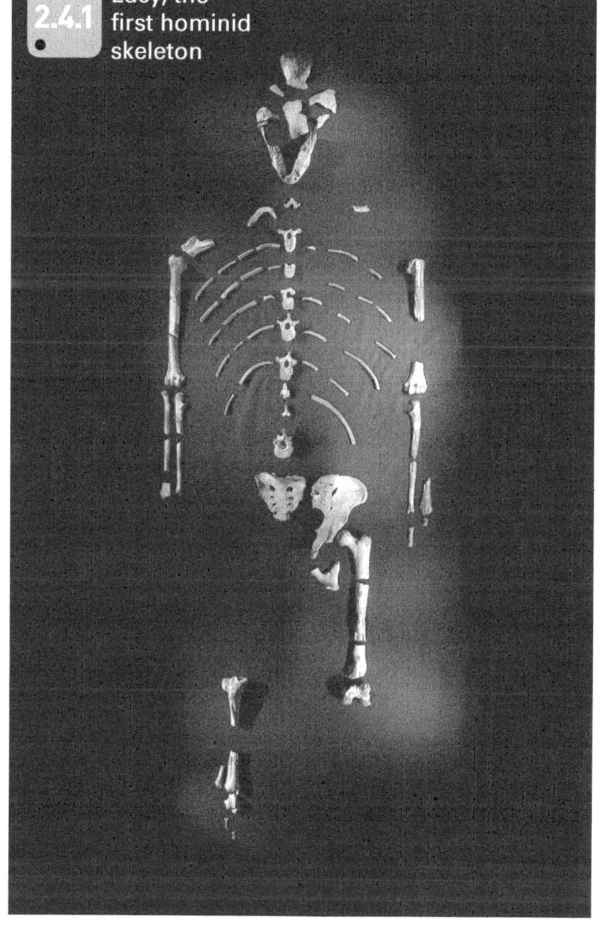

SOURCE 2.4.1 Lucy, the first hominid skeleton

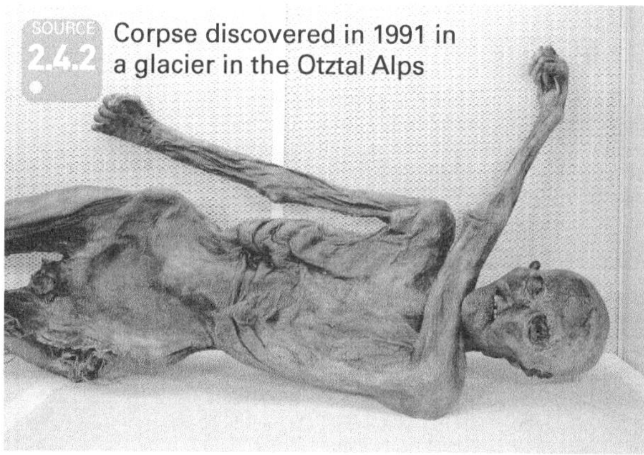

SOURCE 2.4.2 Corpse discovered in 1991 in a glacier in the Otztal Alps

2.5 TIMELINE AND MAPS OF ANCIENT AUSTRALIA

70 000 BC

65 000 BC Signs of human settlement in northern Australia

60 000 BC

60 000 BC Lake Mungo human remains

50 000 BC

45 000 BC Earliest rock engravings, South Australia

40 000 BC

40 000 BC Evidence of settlement at Lake Mungo

30 000 BC

31 000 BC Evidence of settlement west of Melbourne

20 000 BC

10 000 BC

6 000 BC Sea level stabilises at present level

2000 BC

1 AD

2000 AD

1788 AD British colonise Australia, first white settlement

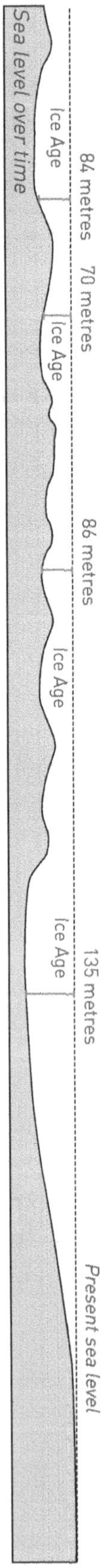

Sea level over time

Ice Age — 84 metres

Ice Age — 70 metres

Ice Age — 86 metres

Ice Age — 135 metres

Present sea level

SOURCE 2.5.1 Timeline of Ancient Australia

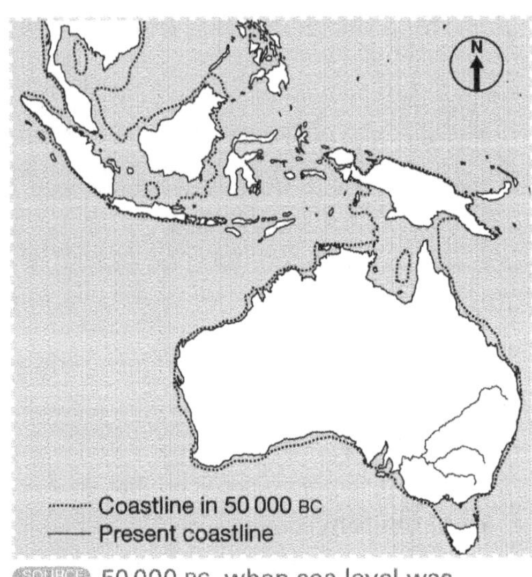

SOURCE 2 50 000 BC, when sea level was 59 metres below present level

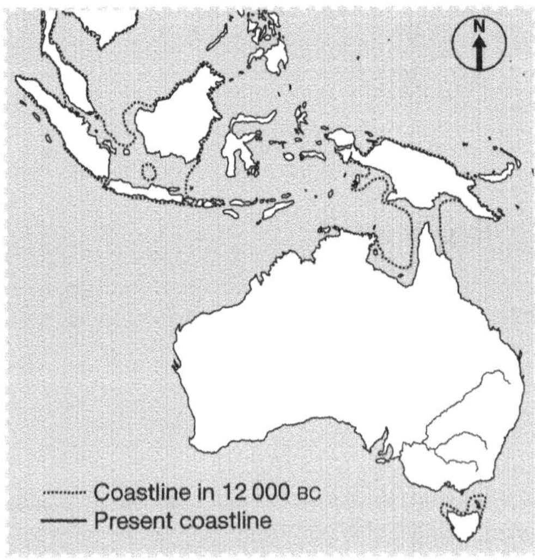

SOURCE 3 12 000 BC, when sea level was 48 metres below present level

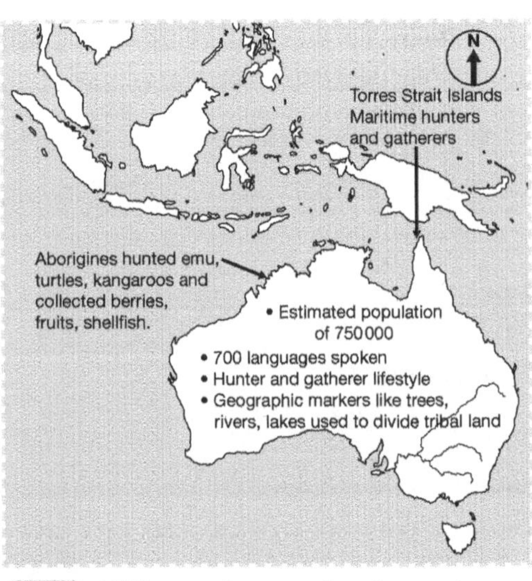

SOURCE 2.5.2 1800 AD, when sea level was at present level

TIMELINE

1 Add the following events to the timeline by placing a coloured dot in the correct location to represent:

- 48 000 BC, when there was first evidence of the creation story *The Rainbow Serpent* (red dot)
- 57 000 BC, when Melanesians settled the Torres Strait Islands (green dot).

MAP OF 50 000 BC

2 Colour the land area of 50 000BC in light green.

3 By what route did the first humans come to Australia?

____

4 If there had not been an Ice Age, how would migration have been affected?

____

____

5 Describe the progress of human settlement across Australia, using two pieces of evidence from the timeline.

____

____

MAP OF 12 000 BC

6 Colour the land area of 12 000BC in light green.

7 What impact would these changes have on further human migration into Australia? Why?

____

____

____

8 When and how were the Torres Strait Islands settled?

____

____

MAP OF 1800 AD

9 What are the two distinct groups of Indigenous people?

____

10 On arrival of the English, what was the estimated population of Indigenous people?

____

11 How many Indigenous language groups were there?

____

2.6 PRIMARY SOURCES: ANCIENT AUSTRALIA

LAND AND KINSHIP

Read the following extracts about the attitudes of Indigenous people to their environment and their family, and answer the questions.

> I feel with my body. Feeling all these trees, all this country. When this blow you can feel it. Same for country … you feel it, you can look, but feeling … that you make.

SOURCE 2.6.1 Bill Neidjie, Gagudju Elder, Kakadu

1 a Which of the five senses is being emphasised in this extract and which sense is inferior in relation to the land?

___

SOURCE 2.6.2 Father Dave Passi, Long Bilong Islander

> It is my father's land, my grandfather's land, my grandmother's land. I am related to it, it give me identity. If I don't fight for it, then I will be moved out of [it] will be the loss of my identity.

b Why do you think Father Passi writes the first line? What message is he trying to get across to the reader?

___

___

c What does he mean when he says 'it give me identity'?

___

___

> All people with the same skin grouping as my mother are my mothers … They have the right, the same as my mother, to watch over me, to control what I'm doing, to make sure that I do the right thing. It's an extended family thing … It's a wonderful secure system.

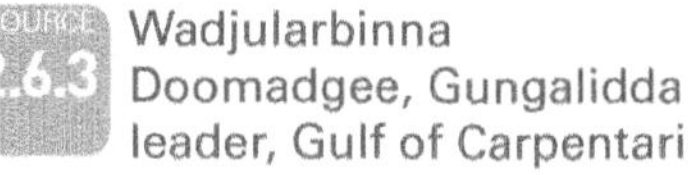
SOURCE 2.6.3 Wadjularbinna Doomadgee, Gungalidda leader, Gulf of Carpentaria

d In Indigenous culture, who cares for the children?

___

e Compare your family set-up with the description above. Is it similar or different? Give two examples from the extract to support your opinion.

___

___

___

___

INDIGENOUS PAINTING

Indigenous people have produced art for thousands of years—rock paintings, rock engravings, body art and bark paintings. Most of their art from the distant past has not survived. Aboriginal art is always connected to the Dreaming.

The Indigenous people have a deep connection with the land. The Dreaming represents their spiritual beliefs. The Dreaming has different meaning for different Aboriginal groups, but for all groups, the Dreaming dominates all aspects of their lives. The Dreaming has all the knowledge and controls all social behaviour and all social structures. It explains the creation of the land and the role of the ancestral spirits.

There is a long tradition of painting on bark. Drawings are made using charcoal on blackened bark. Red, yellow, orange and white were the traditional colours used. Figures were drawn as silhouettes and the designs appear to be X-ray images of their subjects. Bark painting was a part of everyday life.

2 Look at the Indigenous art depicted here and answer the following questions.

a What surface has this painting been done on? How do you know?

____

____

____

____

b Explain whether or not this is an X-ray painting. Give evidence to support your view.

____

____

____

____

c What colours would you expect to see on this painting? Why do you think these are the commonly used colours in Aboriginal art?

____

____

____

____

SOURCE 2.6.4 Aboriginal artist Roderick Maralngurra's bark painting of Naworro, the spirit ancestor of his Ngalngbali clan country, western Arnhem Land. Naworro was a bad spirit man, who killed two of his wives.

d Animals and fish were often the subjects of paintings. Why do you think this was the case?

____

____

____

THE RAINBOW SERPENT: ANCIENT AUSTRALIA

The creation story called *The Rainbow Serpent* is one of the oldest beliefs in the world. While there are many versions of the story, originating from different parts of Australia, there are common elements in all the versions. Here is one version.

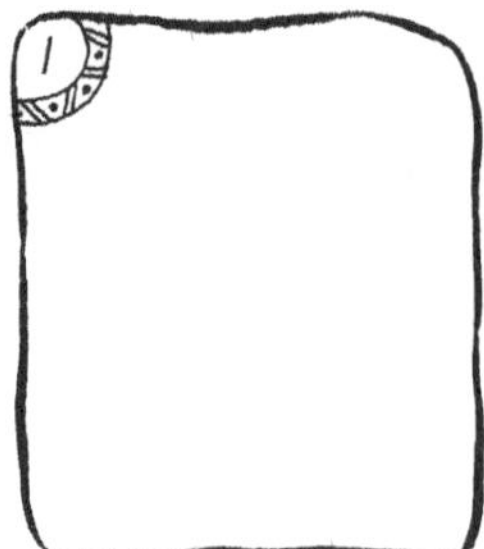

In the beginning the land was a barren plain.

The Rainbow Serpent descended from the visible dark streak in the Milky Way.

The Rainbow Serpent wound his way across the land. His body heaped up mountains and dug out valleys for rivers.

When he had created all the landforms the Rainbow Serpent was tired. He crawled into a waterhole to cool off and sank out of sight.

The Rainbow Serpent shows himself as a rainbow through water and rain.

The Rainbow Serpent can bring good. He has healing powers and knowledge of rain-making.

The Rainbow Serpent can bring evil. He can drown people, bring illness, weakness and death.

SOURCE 2.7.1 The story of the Rainbow Serpent

1 What is the Dreaming?

____

____

2 Look at the 'Timeline and maps of Indigenous history' section in this chapter. How old is the belief in the Rainbow Serpent?

____

3 Where is it believed that the Rainbow Serpent came from?

____

4 How does the Rainbow Serpent reveal himself to people?

____

5 What did the Rainbow Serpent do to gain the respect of the Indigenous people?

____

____

6 Why is the Rainbow Serpent feared?

____

____

7 Complete the story by filling in the first and last drawings.

2.8 CIRCLES AND LINES: ANCIENT AUSTRALIA

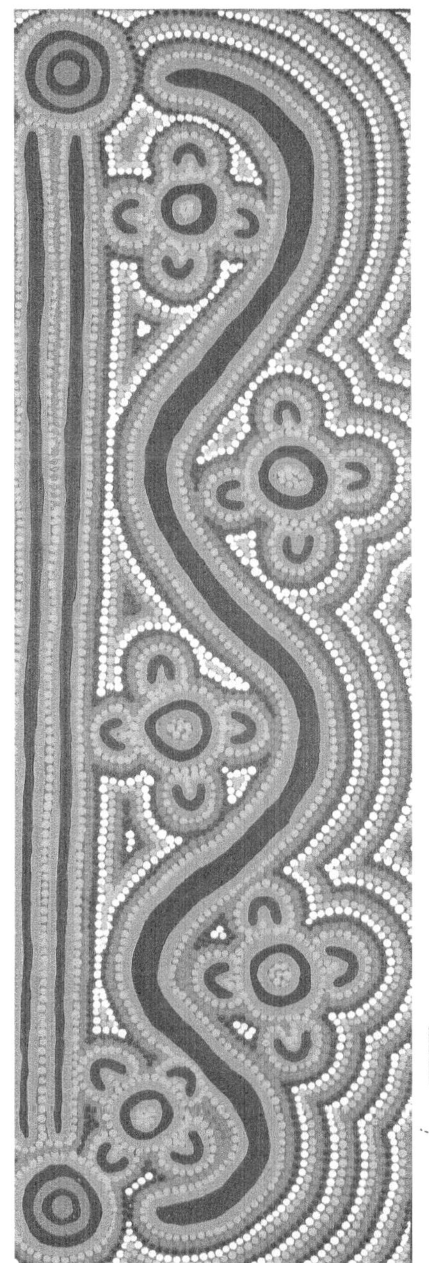

Meaning of the painting: There are twenty people along two creek beds and they are cooking food around five campfires. The painting celebrates the abundance of food.

SOURCE 2.8.1 *Yuendumu* by Brenda Brown

Traditional Indigenous art is not realistic but instead uses symbols. Dots are commonly used to represent stars, sparks and burnt ground. Combinations of symbols are used to give meaning to the painting. The Earth is the basis of all paintings.

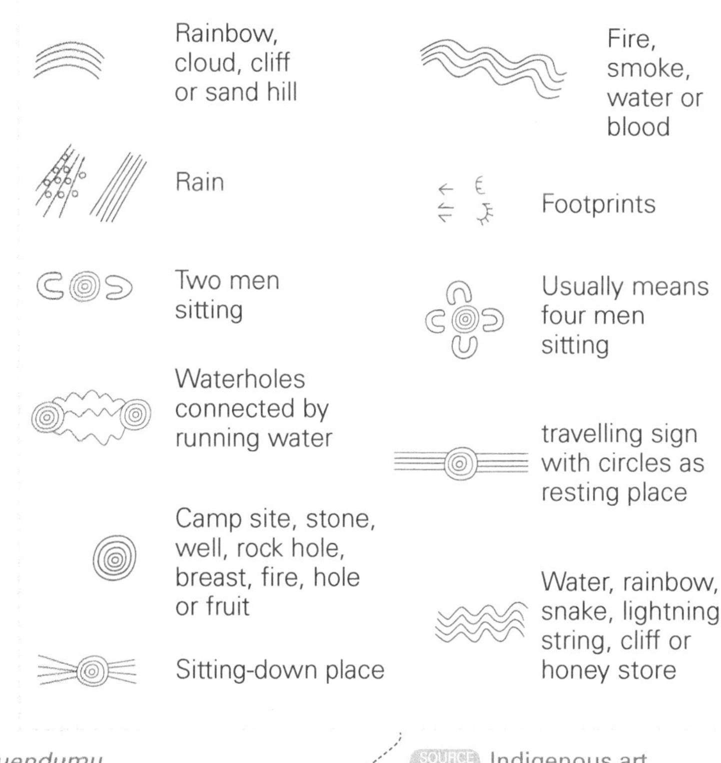

SOURCE 2.8.2 Indigenous art symbols and their meanings

Look at Sources 2.8.1 and 2.8.2. In the space provided below, create your own painting inspired by Indigenous art. Use a minimum of six traditional symbols. Use mainly the traditional colours of red, yellow, orange and white. Add a few other colours if you wish. Annotate the painting to explain the meaning of your art.

TORRES STRAIT ISLANDERS: ANCIENT AUSTRALIA

The Torres Strait Islands stretch 150 kilometres from the northern tip of Queensland to Papua New Guinea. They are a group of 100 islands. The islanders are descendants of Melanesians who migrated there thousands of years ago. These navigators used their canoes to travel from Melanesia to the Torres Strait Islands and to travel between northern Australia and New Guinea for trade. Their knowledge of the constellations and the winds made them a skilled maritime people. They were maritime hunters and gatherers, reaping food from both the land and the sea.

Family has always been an extremely important aspect of life for the Torres Strait Islanders. Look at the drawing below. It uses the coconut tree as a metaphor for their ideas about family. A metaphor is a figure of speech that expresses an idea through the image of another object. Then answer the questions on the following page.

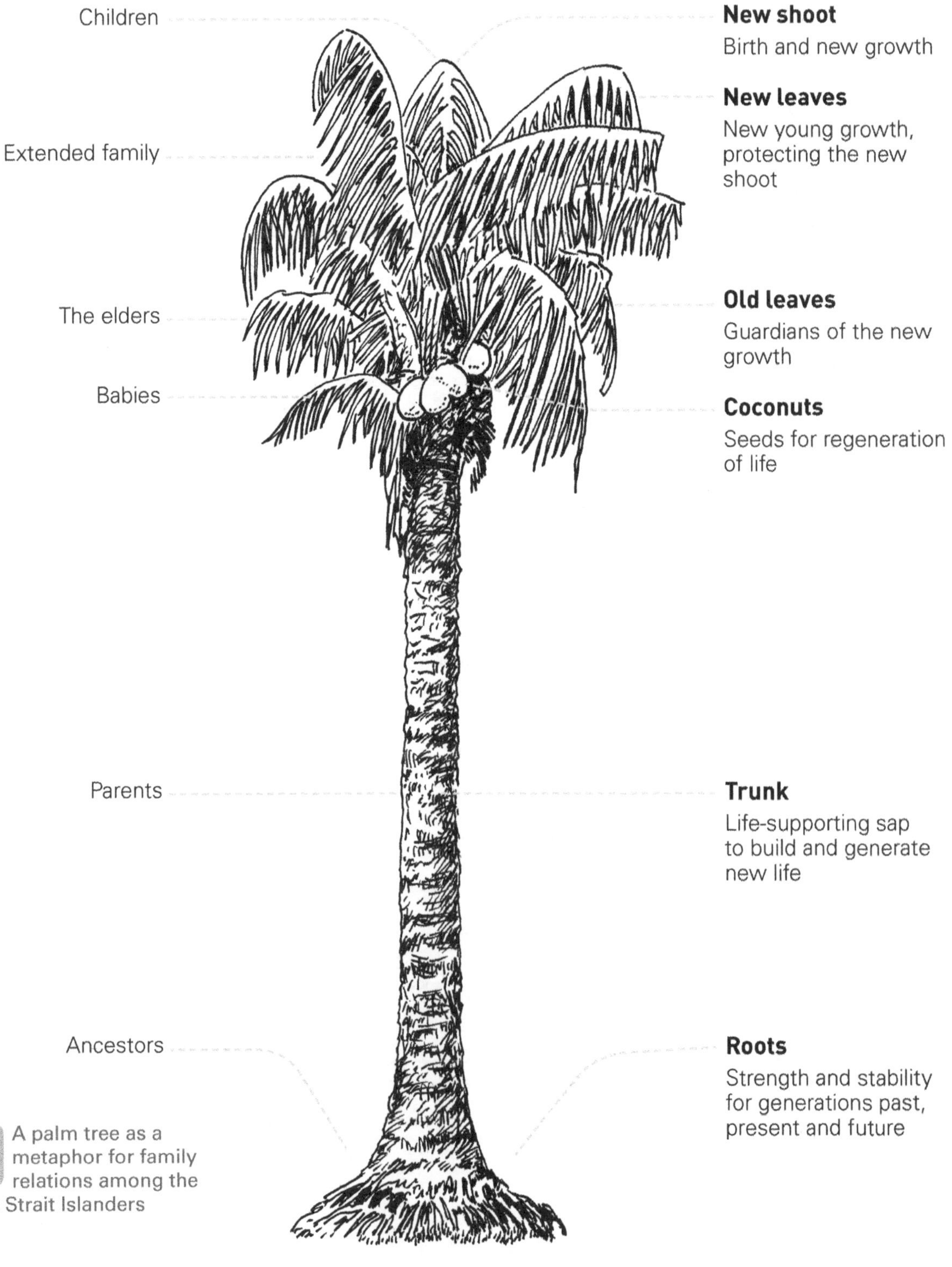

Children — **New shoot**
Birth and new growth

Extended family — **New leaves**
New young growth, protecting the new shoot

The elders — **Old leaves**
Guardians of the new growth

Babies — **Coconuts**
Seeds for regeneration of life

Parents — **Trunk**
Life-supporting sap to build and generate new life

Ancestors — **Roots**
Strength and stability for generations past, present and future

SOURCE 2.9.1 A palm tree as a metaphor for family relations among the Torres Strait Islanders

1 In your own words, explain what a metaphor is.

2 Why do you think a coconut tree is used as the metaphor for family?

3 Which members of the family does this metaphor refer to?

4 Which members of the family do the old, lower leaves represent? What do you think the role of this group is in the family?

5 In this society, who takes responsibility for protecting and teaching the young children?

6 Where do ancestors fit into the metaphor and why are they important?

7 Which part of the coconut tree represents newly born babies in the family?

8 a Explain what Torres Strait Islanders understand by the term 'family'.

b How does the non-Indigenous Australian concept of family compare with that of Torres Strait Islanders? Is it similar or different? How?

TIMELINE OF ANCIENT EGYPT

Refer to the timeline below and conduct research on the internet or in your school library for assistance in completing the following questions.

3000 BC | 2200 | 2000 BC | 1700 | 1100 | 1000 BC | 332 | 1 AD

3000 Egypt unified

3100 Use of hieroglyphics begins

2569 Great Pyramid built

1333 Pharaoh Tutankhamen's rule begins

332 Alexander the Great conquers Egypt

30 Rome conquers Egypt

Old Kingdom | Middle Kingdom | New Kingdom | Different groups of people invade and rule Egypt

SOURCE 3.1.1 Ancient Egypt timeline

1 Colour the different periods of Ancient Egypt's history on the timeline.

2 What event of major importance occurred in 3000 BC? Outline two reasons why this event was so important.

3 Between which years was the Ancient Egyptian civilisation at its peak?

4 When did Ancient Egypt's gradual decline begin? What information provided on the timeline led you to this conclusion?

5 During which period did Pharaoh Tutankhamen live?

6 Add these events to the timeline by placing a coloured dot at the correct location:

- 51 BC Pharaoh Cleopatra VII ascended the throne (red dot).
- 1353 BC Pharaoh Akhenaton ascended the throne (green dot).
- 989 BC Pharaoh Psuesennes I ascended the throne (blue dot).

7 Describe the relationship between Egypt and Rome in 30 BC.

3.2 WRITE LIKE AN EGYPTIAN

The Egyptians developed a type of picture writing called 'hieroglyphics', which means 'sacred writing'. Hieroglyphics was a complicated writing system. The symbols sometimes stood for alphabet sounds, sometimes for syllables and sometimes for objects. There were over 700 hieroglyphs. It is therefore difficult to match hieroglyphs to the letters of the English alphabet. Here is one possible translation, but there are others.

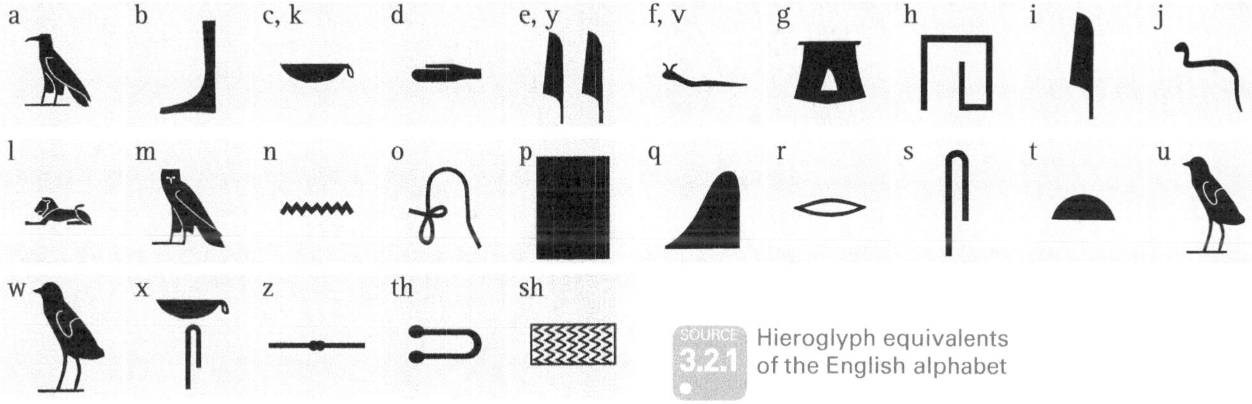

SOURCE 3.2.1 Hieroglyph equivalents of the English alphabet

1 Look carefully at the hieroglyphs and their matching English letters then translate the following statement from hieroglyphs to English.

2 In the box below, translate the following into hieroglyphs:
'The Nile River'.

THE CARTOUCHE

The cartouche was like a modern-day name tag. It was an oblong shape with a horizontal line at one end. A royal name was written on it. Hieroglyphs were written left to right but sometimes they were stacked.

SOURCE 3.2.2 A cartouche of Cleopatra's name

3 Using the information in this section and referring to the sample cartouche for Cleopatra, write your own name in a cartouche.

3.3 MAP OF ANCIENT EGYPT

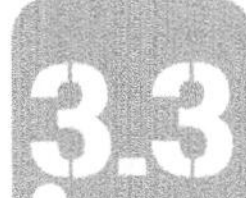

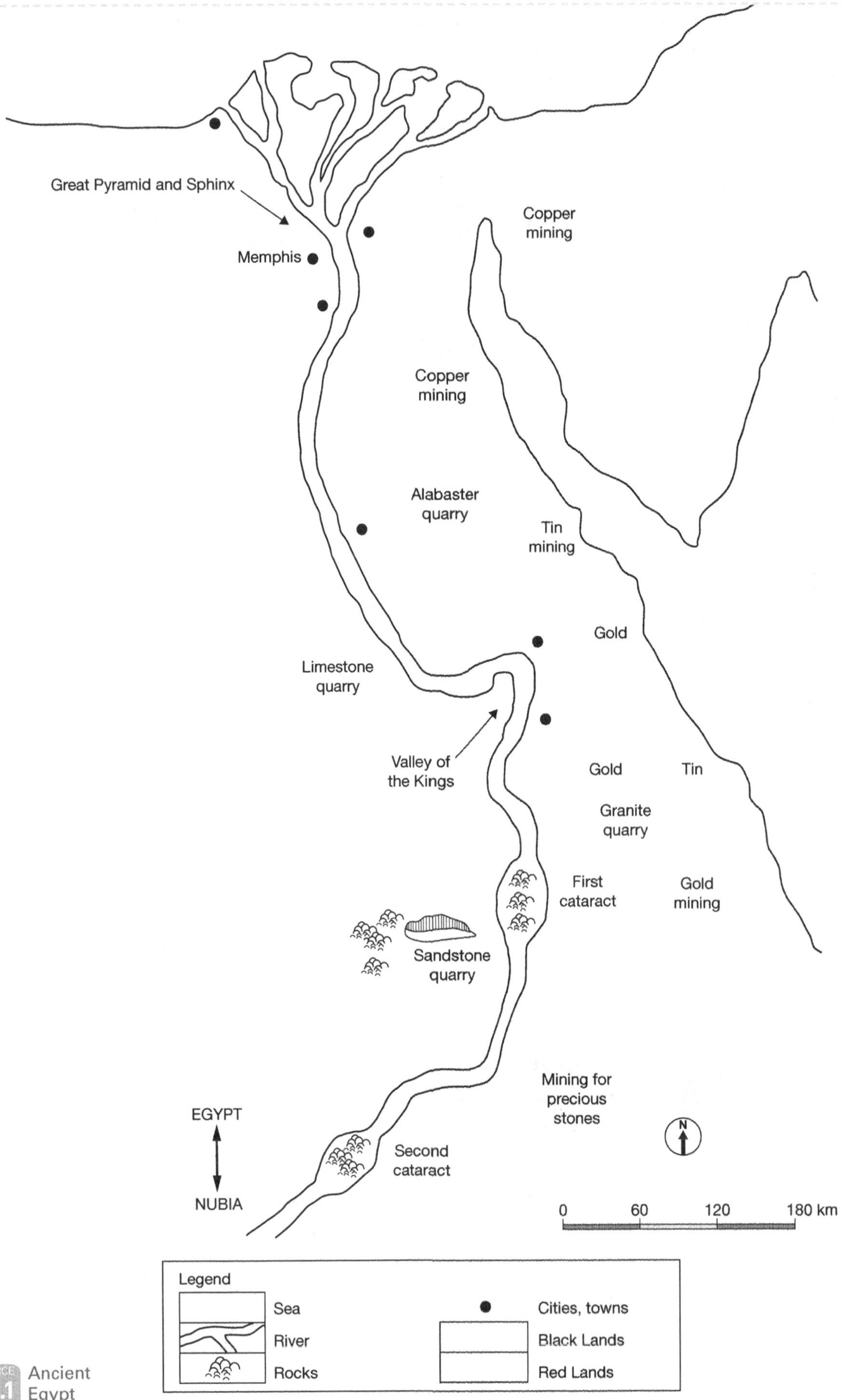

SOURCE 3.3.1 Ancient Egypt

To answer the following questions relating to the map of Ancient Egypt, conduct research on the internet or in your school library.

1 Label the following places on the map:
- Upper Egypt
- Lower Egypt.

2 Name and label Egypt's current capital on the map. Ancient Egypt had ten different capital cities altogether. Label the following three on the map:
- Thebes
- Alexandria
- Akhetaten.

3 Colour and label the following features on the map:
- Nile River
- Red Sea
- Mediterranean Sea
- the Red Lands
- the Black Lands.

Show these colours in the spaces provided in the legend, and label them.

4 Place an arrow near the second cataract to show the direction in which the Nile River flows.

5 Why do you think a large part of Ancient Egypt was given the name the Red Lands?

6 Write a short paragraph to describe the Red Lands. Include reasons why some parts of these lands were occupied.

PRIMARY SOURCES: THE APPRENTICE SCRIBE

Ancient Egypt needed many scribes. They recorded all kinds of information, such as quantities of crops harvested, mathematical calculations for pyramid building, quantities and types of imported and exported products, religious writing in temples and tombs and much more.

See for yourself with your own eye. The occupations lie before you.

The washerman's day is going up, going down. All his limbs are weak, [from] whitening his neighbours' clothes every day, from washing their linen.

The maker of pots is smeared with soil, like one whose relations have died. His hands, his feet are full of clay; he is like one who lives in a bog.

The watchman prepares garlands and polishes vase-stands. He spends a night of toil just as one on whom the sun shines.

The merchants travel downstream and upstream. They are as busy as can be, carrying goods from one town to another. They supply him who has wants. But the tax collectors carry off the gold, that most precious of metals.

The ships' crews from every house [of commerce], they receive their loads. They depart from Egypt for Syria, and each man's god is with him. [But] not one of them says: 'We shall see Egypt again!'.

Imagine this, you are dressed in fine clothes; you own horses. Your boat is on the river; you are supplied with attendants. You stride about inspecting. A mansion is built in your town. You have a powerful office, given you by the pharaoh. Male and female slaves are about you … Put the writings in your heart, and you will be protected from all kinds of toil. You will become a worthy scribe.

SOURCE 3.4.1 An apprentice scribe compares his job with other jobs in Ancient Egypt. The extract is from Papyrus Lansing, twelfth century BC, now held at the British Museum. The photo shows a seated scribe, 25–24th century BC.

1 List all the occupations mentioned.

2 What was the disadvantage of being a washerman?

3 Identify and write two words or phrases used in the extract that make the work of the pot maker appear unpleasant.

4 The description of the potter's work makes reference to an Egyptian death custom. What was that custom?

5 What is a modern-day watchman called? Why do you think the scribe used this as an example of an undesirable job?

6 What did a merchant do to earn his income? What was the disadvantage of this job?

7 What does the scribe mean when he writes of ships' crews that 'not one of them says: "We shall see Egypt again!"'?

8 List all the advantages of earning an income by being a scribe.

3.5 PRIMARY SOURCES: THE NUBIAN SLAVES

1 Who are the people represented in the relief shown below?

SOURCE 3.5.1 Relief of Nubian slaves found in the tomb of the last king of the New Kingdom, Horemheb, who died in 1292 BC. The tomb is located in Saqqara necropolis near Memphis.

2 Where was Nubia in relation to Ancient Egypt? Look at the map in Unit 3.3 of this chapter for help.

3 What do you think the relations between Nubia and Ancient Egypt were like? Why do you think this?

4 Use a Venn diagram to show the similarities and differences between the Egyptians and the Nubians. Refer to paintings of Ancient Egyptians on the internet or in your school library. Consider clothes, adornments, hair styles, facial features and general appearance.

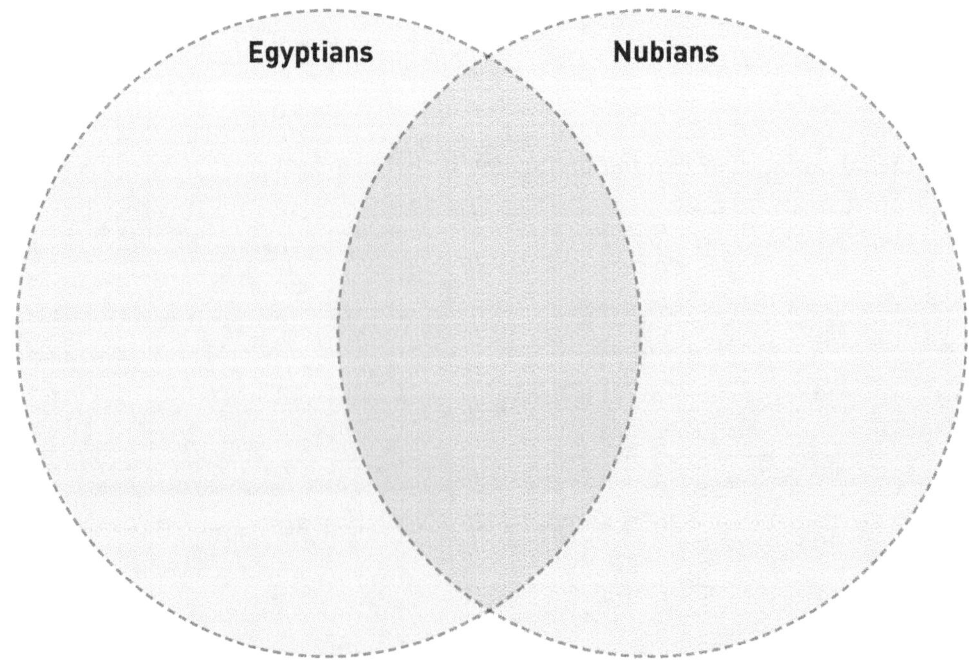

3.6 RECONSTRUCT THE PYRAMID

Triangle A

Triangle A is divided into nine smaller triangles. Each side of the smaller triangles has a clue written on it. The smaller triangles are arranged so that none of the clues match each other.

Triangle B is also divided into nine smaller triangles. Clues are written on the outside of Triangle B.

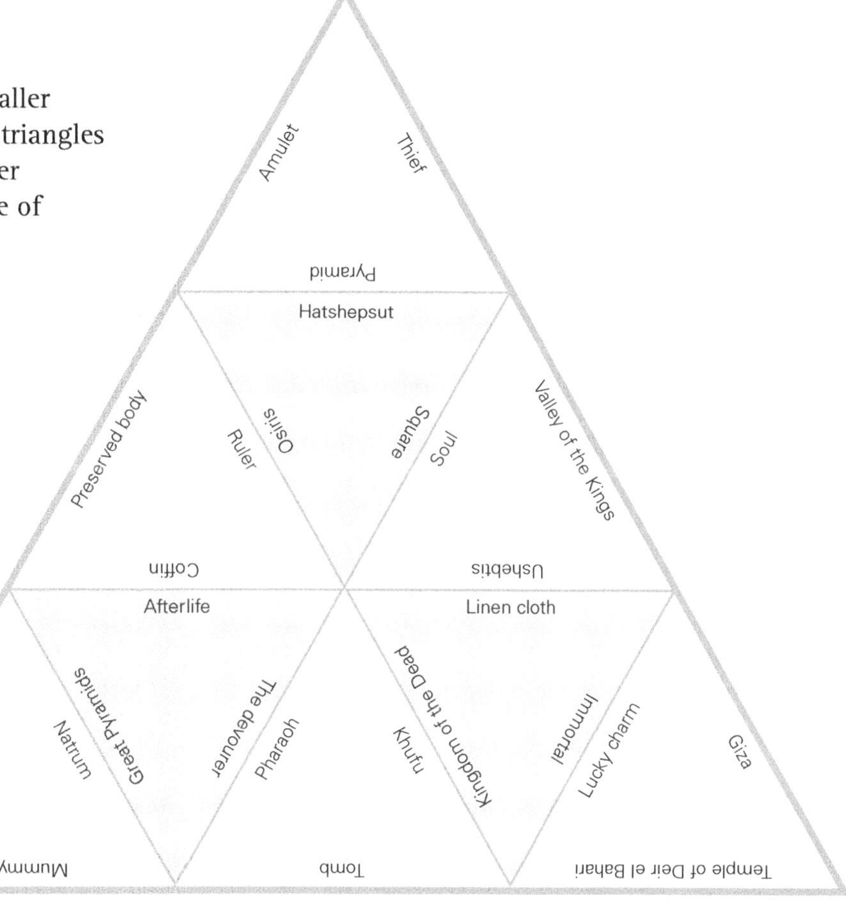

Triangle B

1. Using tracing paper, carefully copy the nine triangles in Triangle A, making sure you include the clues.
2. Cut out the nine small triangles.
3. Place the nine small traced triangles onto Triangle B so that all clues match each other on all sides. The clues on the outer edges of the small triangles should also match the clues on the outside of Triangle B.
4. Once you are sure that the small triangles are positioned correctly, paste them in place.

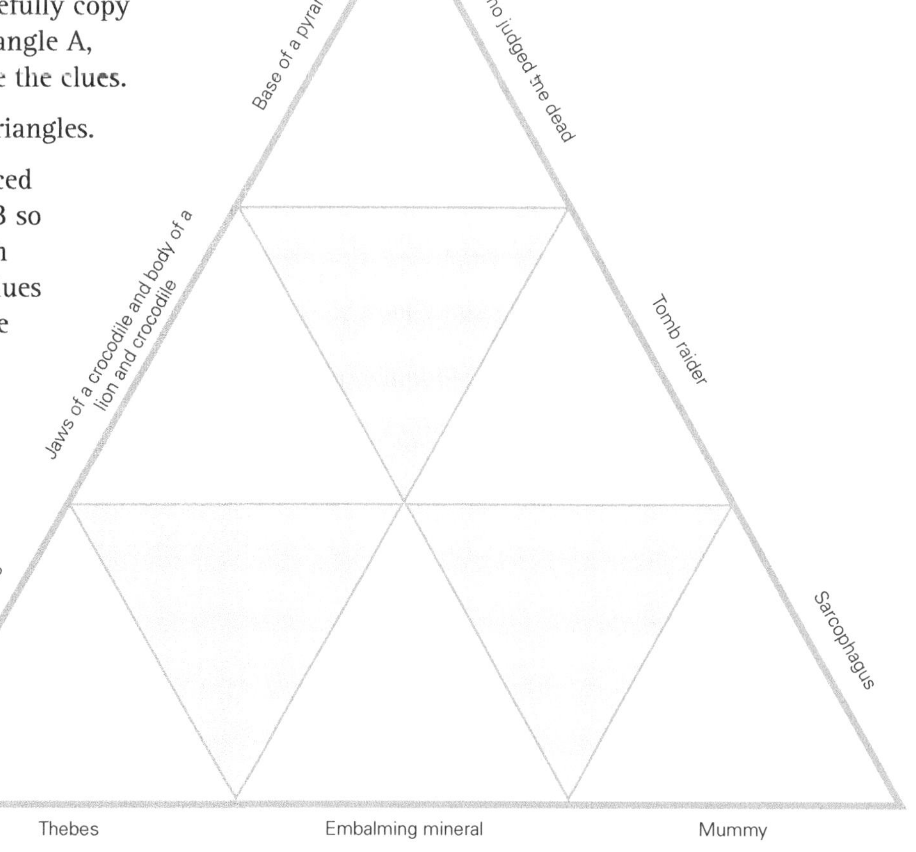

3.7 RICH OR POOR?

1 Below is a jumbled list of sentences about the rich and poor. Identify those that refer to rich Egyptians and highlight them in one colour. Use a different colour to highlight those that refer to poor Egyptians. Refer to the internet or resources in your school library.

- They could not read or write.
- Sacred ceremonies were performed in temples by priests.
- They wore wigs with a block of waxed perfume placed on top of the wig to give off a scent.
- Their mud-brick houses consisted of one or two rooms and had small, high windows to keep out the desert heat.
- Men wore loin cloths and women simple tunics.
- A wide variety of meats were common in their diet.
- Common crafts were pottery, carpentry, stone masonry and jewellery making.
- They lived in large villas of two storeys located along the Nile River.
- They dug the irrigation channels that controlled the Nile's floodwaters and created a favourable farming environment.
- Children were taught farming skills from an early age.
- Boys attended school and learnt to read, write and do arithmetic.
- They prepared and served food for large banquets.
- Hunting wild animals was a popular form of entertainment.
- Children had wooden toys and board games to play with.
- They paid taxes in the form of food.
- Men wore long kilts and women wore pleated dresses. Both sexes wore jewellery.
- Some of them were employed as tomb builders to construct the pharaoh's pyramid.
- They owned beds, chairs, tables, stools, carpets and cushions of woven linen.
- Some of them were employed as scribes who were skilled in writing hieroglyphics.
- They mined for gold and metals in the desert.

2 Imagine you are 10 years old and you have time-travelled back to Ancient Egypt to live with a rich family. Describe one thing you found difficult and one thing you found easy about growing up 3000 years ago.

3 Look at the two drawings below.

a Decide whether they depict wealthy Egyptians or poor Egyptians. Show your answer by clearly labelling the clothing or other symbols that indicate their status.

b Explain the reasons for your decisions in question **a**.

4 Write a paragraph describing four differences between the lives of the rich and the poor in Ancient Egypt.

3.8 REGALIA AND POWER

Throughout history rulers have shown their superior status and importance by wearing and holding special objects. Today, Queen Elizabeth II of Great Britain wears a jewelled crown, purple robes and holds a sceptre on special occasions. Pharaohs were the supreme rulers of Egypt. They were seen as gods with superhuman powers. The pharaohs also had regalia (see below) to show their status.

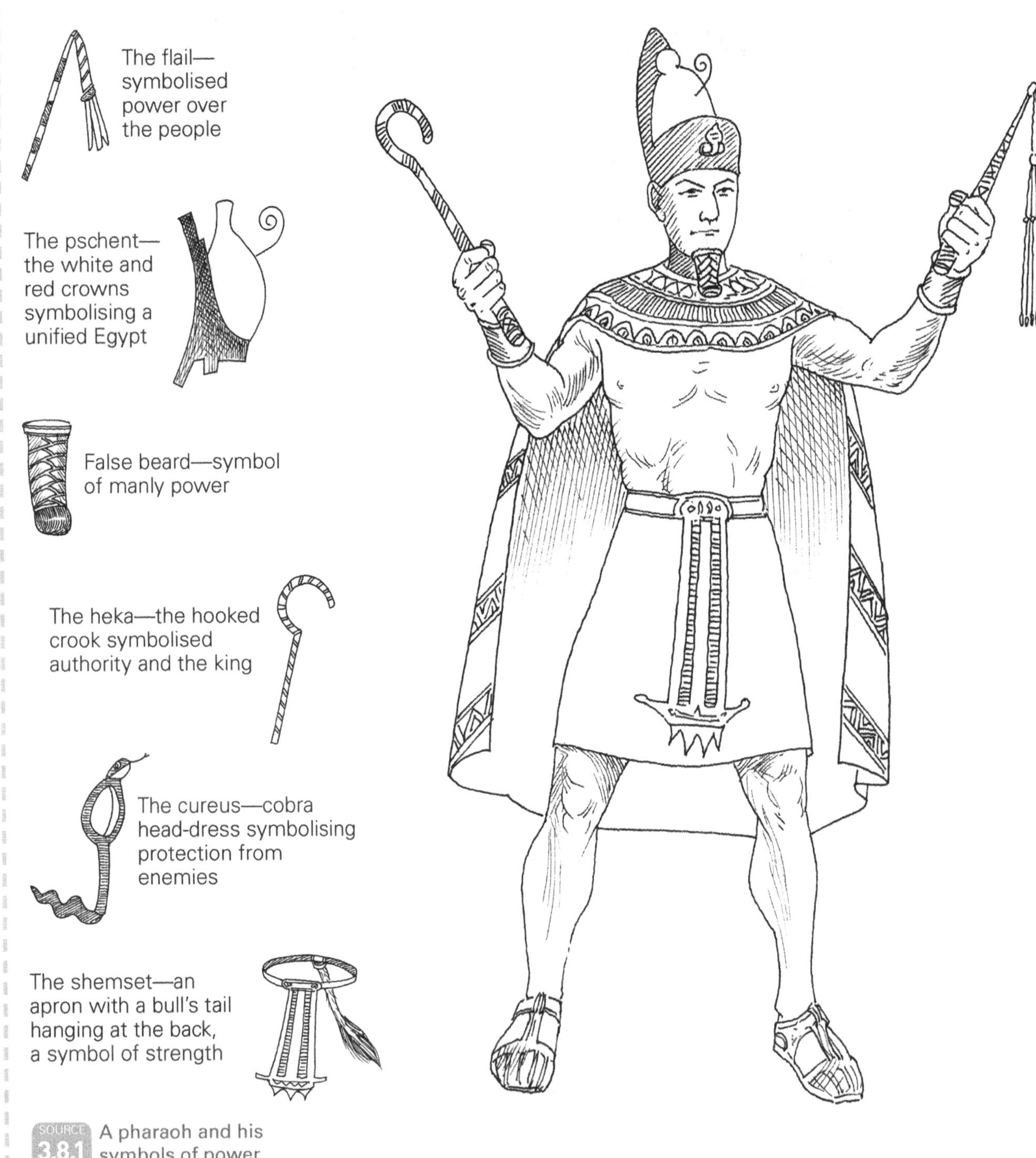

SOURCE 3.8.1 A pharaoh and his symbols of power

1 Look at the drawing of the pharaoh above. Colour and label the objects that show his status.

2 Colour the drawing of the pharaoh, keeping in mind that purple was the colour of royalty and yellows, browns and greens were colours worn by common people.

3 Write a paragraph describing the pharaoh. Include observations about his regalia and dress.

4 In today's world, flags are symbols of their countries. The graphics and colours are carefully designed to give a message about the country. On the Australian flag, for example, the Union Jack shows our links with Britain, the Southern Cross shows Australia's location in the Southern Hemisphere and the seven-pointed Star of Federation represents the states and territories.

Design a flag to represent Ancient Egypt. Include at least three graphics and two colours. Draw the flag in the space provided. Annotate the flag to explain why you selected these colours and graphics.

3.9 THE GODS

Religion was an important part of daily life in Ancient Egypt. It controlled all facets of life for all Egyptians. Religion and superstition went together. Over the years an elaborate creation story grew to explain the origins of the Earth.

1 The following jumbled sentence beginnings and endings, when matched correctly, describe aspects of religion in Ancient Egypt. Match the start of each sentence on the left with its end on the right by colour coding, or draw a line to match the start and end of each sentence. Conduct research on the internet or in your school library to help you.

The Egyptian god who created everything	Egyptians had to cooperate with the gods.
Egyptians believed that	it was a good omen.
Gods were hybrids	listed dreams and their interpretations.
The god of the dead	superstitious and watched out for omens.
During the New Kingdom	was called Anubis.
The Egyptians worshipped	dark and only used by priests.
Temples were built	gods controlled everything in life and death.
Karnak was constructed	Egyptians believed the gods had lost their power.
Temples consisted of	was called Amun-Ra.
The temple's sanctuary was	many animals such as cats.
Egyptians were	to honour the gods.
If an Egyptian dreamt about a large cat	for the god Amun.
The ancient Egyptian Dream Book	with human and animal parts.
To avoid chaos in the world	prayer rooms, granaries and a library.

2 Read the Egyptian creation story below and look at the accompanying illustration. Use this information to:

a label the gods in the illustration

b construct a family tree for the Egyptian gods in the space provided.

In the beginning there was only Nun, a dark water chaos. Out of this rose a hill and on it stood the first god, Atum. When Atum coughed he spat out Shu, the god of air and Tefnut, the goddess of moisture. Shu and Tefnut had two children, Geb the god of the Earth and Nut the goddess of the sky. Shu lifted Nut up so she was a canopy over Geb. Nut and Geb had four children named Osiris, Isis, Seth and Nephthys. Osiris was the king of the Earth and Isis was the queen. Seth's jealousy of Osiris prompted him to kill Osiris. Osiris went to the underworld and Seth became king of the Earth. Horus, the son of Osiris and Isis killed Seth and gained the throne. So it came to be that Horus was king of the Earth and Osiris was king of the underworld.

SOURCE 3.9.1 Egyptian creation story

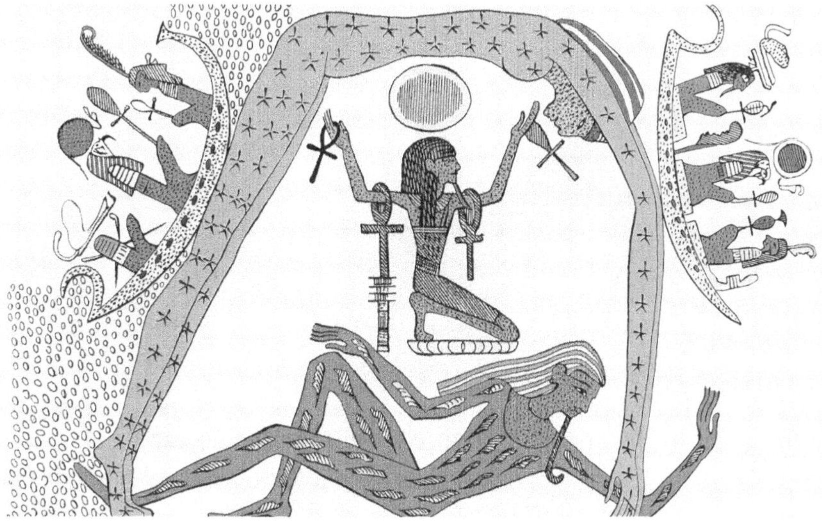

SOURCE 3.9.2 The god of the atmosphere holds up Nut, the goddess of the sky, while standing on Horus, the god of the Earth. Nineteenth-century artwork of a story from the Egyptian creation myths from the third and second millennia BC, from *Pioneers of Science* (Oliver Lodge, 1893).

3.10 THE RHYTHM OF LIFE

1 The three illustrations below show different yearly stages in the cycles, of both humans and nature, along the Nile River. Look carefully at each illustration. Conduct research on the internet or in your school library for information.

In the space adjacent to each illustration:

a name the season

b identify the months of the year when this season occurs

c write four sentences describing the scene.

Season: Months:

Description:

Season: Months:

Description:

Season: Months:

Description:

2 The illustrations are not in the order of the annual events. Starting with the season of least farming activity, number them 1 to 3 to show the annual cycle in order of occurrence. Write your answer in the bottom right box of each answer space.

3.11 MAKING MUMMIES

The Ancient Egyptians did things a little differently from us today. They had some very different beliefs and customs when it came to death. Look carefully at the drawing of a pharaoh in the process of undergoing mummification.

The whole process can be seen as having three parts:

1 Preparation before working on the body

2 Preparing the body

3 Preserving the body

Read the list of jobs below, that the embalmers did when making mummies. Decide which part of the mummification process (part 1, 2 or 3 above) each job slots into. Use colour coding to highlight your answers. For example, you might use yellow to indicate 'Preparation before working on the body'.

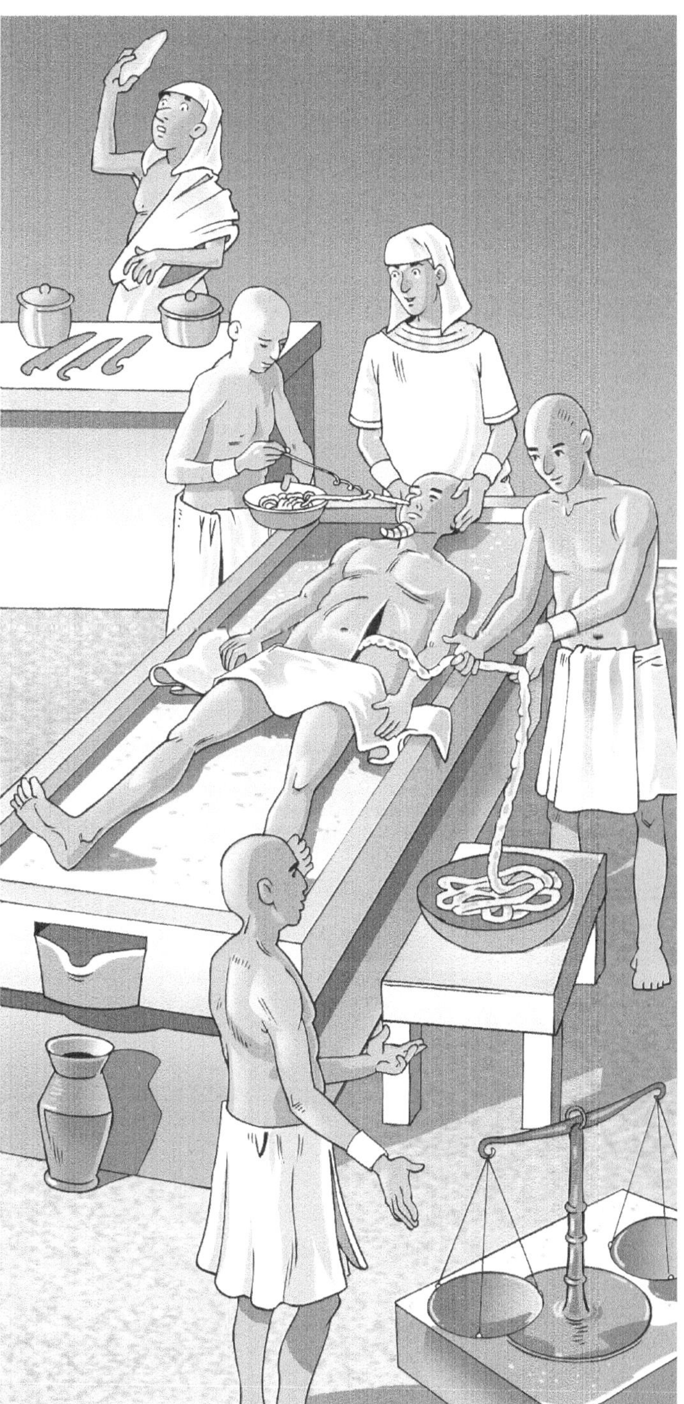

- Pull out brain through nostrils
- Sharpen implements for cutting open the flesh
- Wash internal organs, dry them and wrap in linen
- Bandage whole body with linen
- Obtain Canopic jars
- Pack brain cavity with linen
- Cut open the chest
- Leave the body for about 15 days
- Remove the heart
- Soak body in natron
- Remove internal organs
- Get bags of natron
- Pack eye sockets with linen
- Stuff body with bags of natron and resin-soaked bandages
- Obtain at least 7 metres of the finest linen
- Wash the heart, dry it and return to chest cavity
- Place internal organs in Canopic jars

CHAPTER 4: ANCIENT GREECE

TIMELINE OF ANCIENT GREECE

In the space provided, prepare a timeline to show the key events listed below that occurred in Ancient Greece between the years 2500 BC and 641 AD. Place these key events in their correct position on the timeline and clearly label them. It may be helpful to first reorganise the list in chronological order.

- 461 BC First Peloponnesian War between Athens and Sparta
- 480 BC Classical period begins
- 146 BC Rome conquers Greece
- 267 AD Goths attack Greece
- 800 BC Age of colonisation begins
- 641 AD Slavic tribes take over Greece
- 449 BC Building of Parthenon starts
- 338 BC Hellenistic period begins
- 776 BC First Olympic Games
- 2500 BC Minoan civilisation emerges on Crete

TRUE OR FALSE?

Indicate whether the following statements about Ancient Greece are true or false. Conduct research on the internet or in your school library to help you.

	TRUE OR FALSE?
The word 'Greece' is a Roman word.	
Greece is a mountainous country in which transport was difficult in ancient times.	
The Aegean civilisations were the earliest Greek civilisations.	
Socrates was a famous Spartan philosopher.	
Democracy was developed in Corinth during the Classical period.	
Greek city-states emerged during the period of Colonisation.	
Only men performed in Greek dramas.	
The Minoan civilisation was located in the Peloponnese.	
Dionysus, the god of wine, was celebrated annually in an Athenian festival.	
All the following words linked to the theatre are Greek words: drama, chorus, actor, orchestra and make-up.	
Philosophers are people who perform in the theatre.	
Socrates was found guilty of corrupting young Athenians and disrespecting the gods.	
Sparta was the most powerful city-state in the period immediately following the Persian Wars.	
In philosophy, the study of right and wrong is called ethics.	
Socrates was stabbed to death by Athenians who disapproved of his teachings.	
Plays were first performed in Athens in the mid-fifth century BC.	
The chorus took part in plays in the theatre by making comments on what was happening in the play.	
Amphitheatres were large enclosed and roofed structures in which plays were performed.	

THE GEOGRAPHY OF ANCIENT GREECE

The geography of Ancient Greece played a very significant part in its history. Mountains, valleys and seas all influenced where settlements grew and how people travelled between them. Complete the tasks below to gain a greater understanding of the relationship of geography and history.

SOURCE 4.3.1 Greece

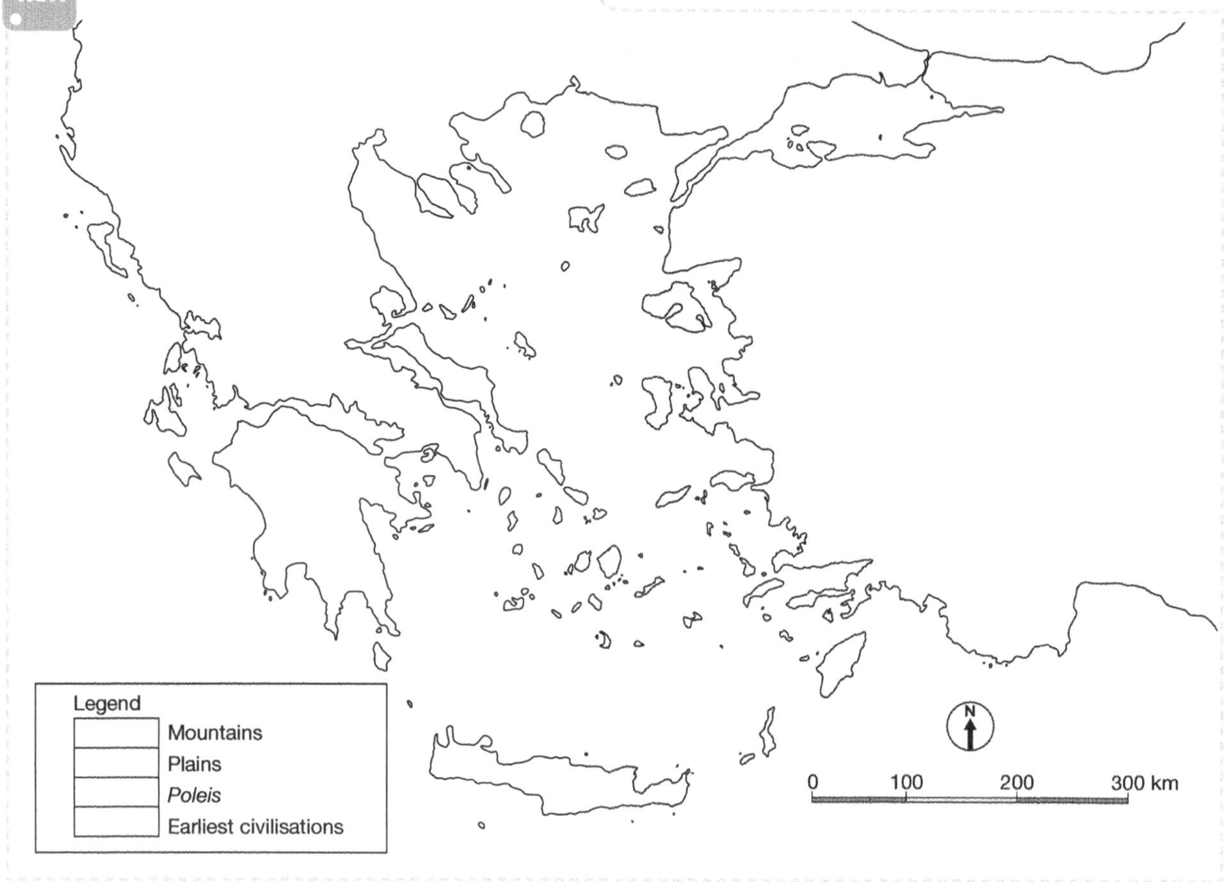

Legend
Mountains
Plains
Poleis
Earliest civilisations

N

0 100 200 300 km

1 Use the above map to complete the following activities. On the internet or in your school library, find a map of Ancient Greece to help you.

- **a** Ancient Greece was divided into city-states or *poleis*. Mark and label the poleis of Athens, Sparta, Thebes, Olympia, Thermopylae and Corinth on the map. Indicate the symbol and colour used to represent the *poleis* in the legend.
- **b** Mark and label the earliest civilisations at Knossos and Mycenae. Indicate the symbol and colour used in the legend.
- **c** Label the seas, oceans and Mount Olympus.
- **d** Colour in the location of the mountains. Indicate the colour used in the legend.
- **e** Look in an atlas at a map of Greece. Locate the main plains and colour them on the map. Indicate the colour used in the legend.
- **f** Write a suitable title for the map.

2 a Describe the location of the main *poleis* in relation to the landscape.

b Why were these sites selected for the *poleis*?

3 Explain one advantage and one disadvantage of the location of the *poleis*.

4 Ancient Greece was never united under one government. Explain what part the geography of Greece played in keeping the city-states separate.

5 Indicate whether the following statements are true or false.

	TRUE OR FALSE?
Knossos was the most southern Ancient Greek city.	
Delphi was located near Mount Olympus.	
The cities of Athens and Marathon faced the Ionian Sea.	
Sparta and Athens were no more than 100 kilometres distance from each other.	
Sparta was one of three cities of the Peloponnese.	
Troy was located north-east of Athens, in Asia Minor.	
Athens was located in the region called Attica.	
Mount Parnassus separated the cities of Thermopylae and Marathon.	

PRIMARY SOURCES

THE OLIGARCH

1 Read the following extract.

> I object to this form of government because it means that the interests of the mob are more important than those of respectable people. Throughout the whole world, aristocracy is opposed to democracy; for aristocracy means discipline, obedience to the laws and concern for what is respectable. On the other hand, the common people are ignorant, ill-disciplined and immoral. However, it is appropriate that in Athens the poor and the common people should seem to have more power than the noble and the rich, because it is this class that provides the rowers for the fleet and on which the power of the city is based.

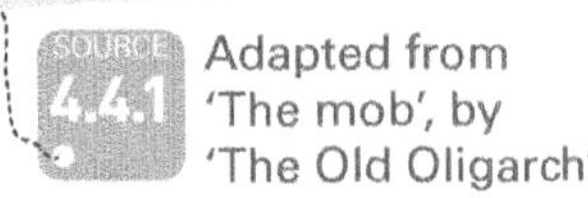

Adapted from 'The mob', by 'The Old Oligarch'

a Do the Oligarchs like or dislike democracy? Give one piece of evidence from the extract that supports your answer.

____

____

____

b The document states that one group of Athenians are 'respectable'. To which social group is the Oligarch group referring?

____

____

c What were the characteristics of 'respectable' Athenians, according to the extract?

____

____

____

d What name was given to common Athenians? Is this a compliment or an insult? Explain your answer.

____

____

____

____

e What reasons are given for the common people being unsuitable to hold power?

____

____

f To which social group do you think the Oligarch belong and why?

g From this extract, what do you understand democracy to be?

POTTERY

Greek pottery was functional and artistically beautiful. The designs and drawings on pottery give an insight into life in Ancient Greece.

2 Look carefully at the amphora below and complete the tasks.

SOURCE 4.4.2 Athenian black figure amphora showing olive gathering, c. 520 BC

a Select labels from the list below and place them in the correct boxes to describe the amphora.

- olive tree
- man collecting olives
- geometric pattern
- man in olive tree shaking branches
- man with stick hitting branches

b What is happening in the scene painted on the pottery?

c Why do you think that the product that is being farmed was important enough to be the topic for decorating the pottery?

THE PERSIAN WARS

The Persian Wars united the Greek city-states against a common foreign enemy. Key events are shown on the timeline. A map shows important locations of the wars.

Carefully study the timeline and map to answer the questions.

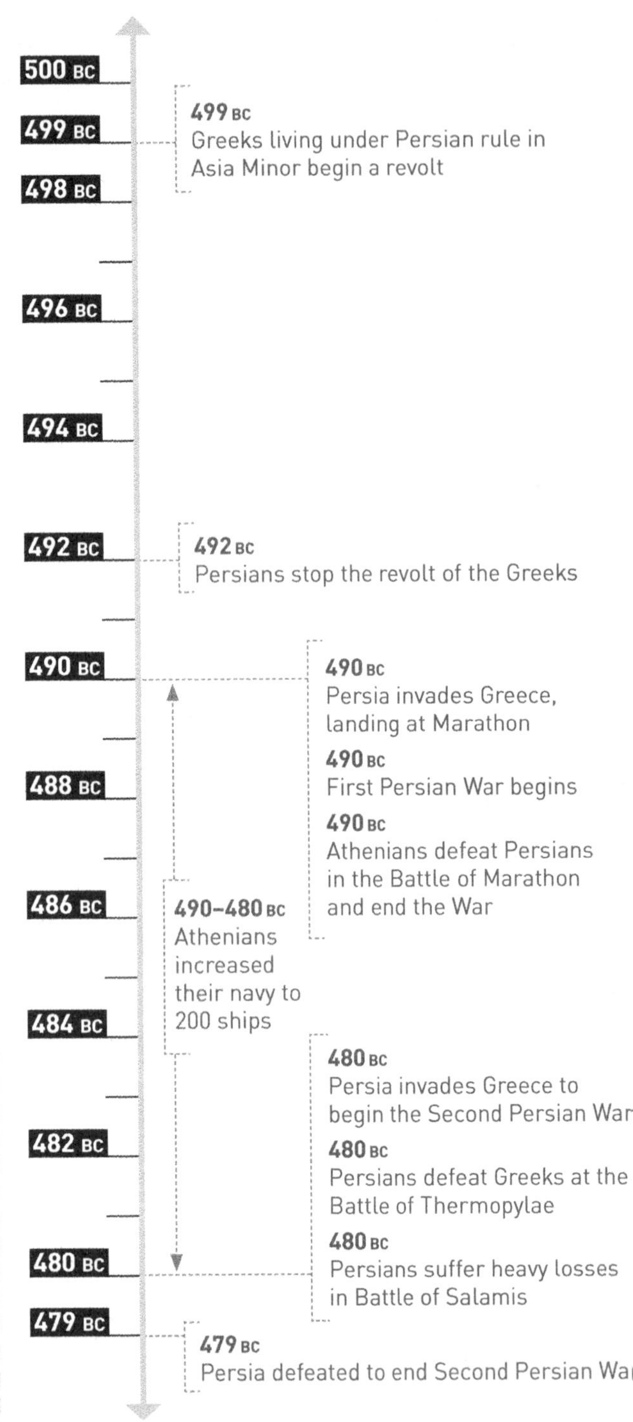

SOURCE 4.5.1 Timeline of the Persian Wars

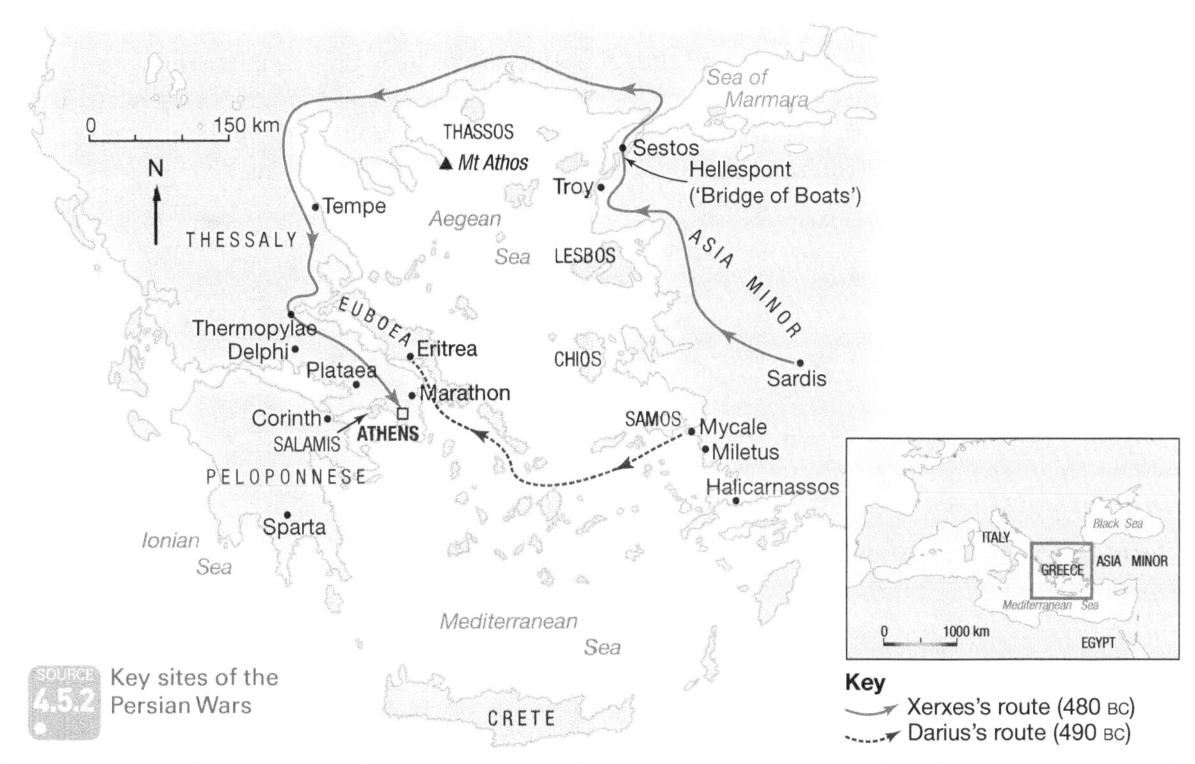

SOURCE 4.5.2 Key sites of the Persian Wars

1 How long was it from the start of the First Persian War and the end of the Second Persian War?

2 How did the Greeks try to improve their defence after the First Persian War?

3 During which Persian War did the Battle of Thermopylae occur?

4 Explain why Persian invasions focused on eastern Greece.

5 What signs were there before war broke out, that relations between Persia and Greece were not good?

4.6 SPARTANS AND ATHENIANS

1 Conduct research on the internet and the school library to help you complete the following questions. Below is a jumbled list of words, phrases and sentences that relate to Athenians and Spartans. Identify all those that relate to Athenians and highlight in one colour. Use a different colour to highlight all those that relate to Spartans.

Acropolis	children had toys and games
all land was state-owned	children's lives were controlled by the State
boys at 7 began their education in reading, writing and arithmetic	Ephebic Oath
boys were taught music and poetry	Eupatrids
children were deliberately deprived of food	girls were trained in physical fitness
stealing was considered a virtue	girls were taught household chores
thinking and philosophy were highly regarded	Herlots
training of boys aimed to toughen them	honourable to die in battle
weak babies were left to die	metrics
Perioiki	military training started at 7 for boys
slaves	outsiders unwelcome
Spartiates	Parthenon
people spent much time in the agora	

2 Imagine you are a Spartan child who has been taken to live with an Athenian family. Describe two immediate changes you must make in your behaviour. Why must you make these changes?

3 a Look at the two illustrations below. Decide which drawing would be typical of a Spartan and which of an Athenian. Show your answer by clearly labelling each drawing.

______________________ ______________________

b Explain the reasons for your decision in the previous question.

____

____

____

____

____

____

4 Write a paragraph describing four differences between life in Athens and life in Sparta.

____

____

____

____

____

____

____

____

GENERATIONS OF GODS

The Ancient Greeks created a complex mythology of gods with extraordinary powers. The god Uranus and goddess Gaia were the first immortals to rule in the Golden Age. Their children were the Titan gods. Titans were overthrown by a younger generation of gods that became known as the Olympians. It is the twelve gods of Mount Olympus that are possibly the best known of all the Greek gods.

THE GENERATIONS OF GODS IN ANCIENT GREEK MYTHOLOGY.

These are some of the most important gods. There were many others, especially when the first generation of Olympians had children.

	GODS	GODDESSES
Golden Age	Uranus (Heaven)	Gaia (Earth)
Titan gods: First generation	Oceanus Hyperion Coeus Kronos Crius Iapetus	Mnemosyne Tethys Theia Phoebe Rhea Themis
Titan gods: Second generation	Prometheus Atlas Epimetheus Calypso Menoetius Atraeus Pallas Perses Helios	Leto Asteria Metis Eos Selene
Olympian gods: First generation	Zeus Poseidon Dionysus Apollo Hermes Ares Hephaestus	Athena Hera Demeter Artemis Aphrodite

SOURCE 4.7.1 An Etruscan black-figure vase painting of Prometheus.
The generations of gods in Ancient Greek mythology.
These are some of the most important gods. There were many others, especially when the first generation of Olympians had children.

1 Read the unfinished story of Prometheus below and complete it by writing in the correct word from the list provided. This is one version of the story but there are other variations of the same basic myth.

- heaven
- arrested
- feast
- war
- Zeus
- angry
- suffering
- liver
- advised
- Titan
- stomach
- revenge
- torture
- conflict
- power
- chains
- king
- Prometheus
- forethought
- fire

Prometheus was a ____________________ god. His name means to think ahead, or ____________________. Prometheus was given the task of creating humans out of clay. His protection of the humans he created brought him into ____________________ with Zeus. Before the time when Zeus ruled the gods, there were struggles for ____________________ in the heavens. A group of young gods stirred to remove Kronos and replace him with ____________________ as ruler. Prometheus attempted to prevent violence and

____________________ by encouraging peaceful discussions, but no one listened. Eventually he took the part of Zeus and ____________________ him how to become ruler of the gods. Kronos and his supporters were exiled to a cave in Tartarus.

It was said by the Ancient Greeks that once at Mecone, Prometheus set out to deceive Zeus. ____________________ tricked Zeus out of the best part of the sacrificial ____________________, so kept the best meat for humans. He cut up a bull and divided it into two parts. He wrapped the best portions in skins and placed the worst part, the ____________________ on the top. The second part was made of the bones covered with fat. Prometheus asked Zeus to choose which part he preferred. Zeus was ____________________ at the choices. He selected the bones. Zeus was furious and avenged himself by taking fire away from humans. Prometheus responded by stealing ____________________ back again. He used a hollow tube of a fennel stalk to take fire from ____________________ and give it back to humans for their benefit. Prometheus is credited for giving fire to humans.

Zeus, the ____________________ of all gods, was outraged! He called on Hephaestus to use earth to make a woman. He called upon Athena to give this woman all the charms to entice humans so they would accept her amongst them. The woman was named Pandora and was the ____________________ of Zeus on humans. Pandora, upon succumbing to temptation and lifting the lid of the box Zeus had forbidden her to open, released diseases and all sorts of ____________________ and misfortunes on humans.

Zeus also took revenge on Prometheus. He was ____________________ and taken to the Caucasus Mountains where he was chained to a pillar. Zeus sent an eagle to feast on Prometheus's ____________________. All day the eagle ate and at night the liver regenerated. Prometheus experienced perpetual ____________________ for years until Heracles killed the eagle and released Prometheus from his ____________________________.

2 Complete the following tasks using information from this unit.

a Who were the grandparents of Prometheus?

____

b Describe one similarity and one difference between Zeus and Prometheus.

____

____

c List three things you learnt about the Greek gods from the story of Prometheus.

____

____

d What part of the Prometheus story does source 4.7.1 depict?

____

____

4.8 ORACLES AND PROPHECIES

The Ancient Greeks believed the future could be seen by oracles or prophets. The most famous oracle was at Delphi. The oracle sat next to a fissure in the ground from which cold vapours emerged. She went into a trance as she made a prophecy. When the oracle uttered words, a priest would interpret what was uttered. The Greeks sought prophecies on private matters as well as political matters. The oracle was seen as someone with special powers to speak on behalf of the gods.

Read the following story involving prophecies by oracles. This story was written as a play by Sophocles and was first performed in 429 BC. Sophocles named the play *Oedipus Rex*, or *Oedipus the King*.

Laius and Jocasta, King and Queen of Thebes, have a baby boy.

An oracle prophesies that the boy will kill his father and marry his mother.

To prevent the prophecy from coming true, the baby is abandoned in the mountains to die.

A shepherd finds the baby and takes him home to Corinth. He names the baby Oedipus and adopts him as his son.

As a young man, Oedipus visits the oracle at Delphi and is told he will kill his father and marry his mother.

To prevent the prophecy from eventuating, Oedipus leaves his home.

While travelling Oedipus gets in a squabble with a stranger and kills him. The stranger is his father.

Further along his journey Oedipus solves the riddle of the Sphinx and so frees the Kingdom of Thebes.

Oedipus frees Thebes from the curse and as a reward he is crowned king. He marries the widowed queen without realising she is his mother. The prophecy is fulfilled.

From the story and information above answer the following questions.

1 What was an oracle?

2 Who were Laius and Jocasta?

3 What prophecy did an oracle make about the baby prince?

4 After hearing the oracle's prediction, what action did Laius and Jocasta take and why?

5 Explain why Oedipus was raised by adoptive parents.

6 Why did a prophecy by the oracle of Delphi cause Oedipus to leave home?

7 Explain how the prophecies came to be fulfilled when both King Laius and Oedipus took action to prevent the events happening.

8 Oedipus solved the riddle of the Sphinx. Can you? What do you think is the answer to the riddle? The correct answer can be found at the end of this chapter.

What creature walks on four legs in the morning, two legs at noon and three legs in the evening?

IT'S ALL GREEK TO ME!

There are hundreds of words in the English language derived from Greek. You may speak some Greek without even realising it.

1 Below is a list of English words, the Greek roots from which they are derived, and their meanings. Complete the list by writing five other English words derived from Greek roots. You can use the same roots shown in the list. Give a meaning for each of the words you write in the right-hand column.

ENGLISH WORD	GREEK ROOT	MEANING
Archaeology	*archaeo* = ancient, beginning *logy* = word, knowledge	Study of ancient cultures
Monologue	*mono* = single, one *logue* = word	Long speech made by one person
Thermometer	*thermo* = temperature *meter* = measurement	Instrument that measures temperature
Astronaut	*astro* = star *naut* = sailor	Person who travels in outer space
Psychiatrist	*psych* = soul, spirit, workings of the mind *iatrist* = healer, doctor	Doctor who deals with diagnosis and treatment of mental disorders
Autobiography	*auto* = self *bio* = life *graphy* = to write	Account of a person's life written by that person
Microscope	*micro* = tiny, small *scope* = to look at	Instrument for looking at tiny objects and magnifying them
Pentathlon	*pent* = five *athlon* = athletic	Athletic sport of five activities in the one competition
Neolithic	*neo* = new *lithic* = stone	Historical period, also called the New Stone Age
Geometry	*geo* = earth *metry* = measurement	Topic in mathematics that involves measurement of the Earth's surface

The Ancient Greek words that have been absorbed into the English language were originally written in Greek. The Greeks had their own alphabet. All writing was in upper case as lower case letters had not been invented.

GREEK ALPHABET		ENGLISH LETTER	ENGLISH PRONUNCIATION	GREEK ALPHABET		ENGLISH LETTER	ENGLISH PRONUNCIATION
Α	alpha	A	about	Ν	nu	N	not
Β	beta	B	very	Ξ	xi	X	exit
Γ	gamma	G	yell	Ο	omicron	O	four
Δ	delta	D	than	Π	pi	P	petal
Ε	epsilon	E	egg	Ρ	rho	R	rice
Ζ	zeta	Z	zoo	Σ	sigma	S	salad
Η	eta	H	igloo	Τ	tau	T	talent
Θ	theta	TH	thistle	Υ	upsilon	U	igloo
Ι	iota	I	igloo	Φ	phi	PH	false/photo
Κ	kappa	K	cake	Χ	chi	CH	huff
Λ	lambda	L	lamp	Ψ	psi	PS	epsom salts
Μ	mu	M	mum	Ω	omega	O	four

2 **a** Look at the example below then sound out the Greek word and write it phonetically. Finally, write the word in English. For example:

[Greek] ΧΑΡΙ ΠΟΤΕΡ

[Sounds like] HARI POTER

[English] HARRY POTTER

b Now write the following place name in English: ΑΥΣΤΡΑΛΙΑ

____

3 **a** Look at the Greek and matching English letters of the alphabet in the following example.

[English] MICHELLE JOHNSON

[Sounds like] MICHEL JONSON

[Greek] ΜΙΣΕΛ ΓΟΝΣΟΝ

b Write your full name in English. Sound out your name and write it phonetically. Translate your name into Greek by matching the letters as closely as possible.

____

____

____

____

Answer: Human beings. As babies (morning), humans crawl on hands and knees; as adults (noon), humans walk on two feet; and in old age (evening), they walk with the aid of a walking stick, which is the third leg.

LOCATION OF ANCIENT ROME

1 Complete the following tasks on the outline map. Refer to an atlas and conduct some research on the internet or in your school library for assistance.

- **a** Colour the area that made up the Roman Empire at its maximum size. Show this colour in the space provided in the legend and label it.
- **b** Shade the area outside the Roman Empire in a different colour. Label and colour in the legend in the space provided.
- **c** Label the seas and oceans.
- **d** Show the position of the city of Rome and label it.
- **e** Write a suitable title for the map.

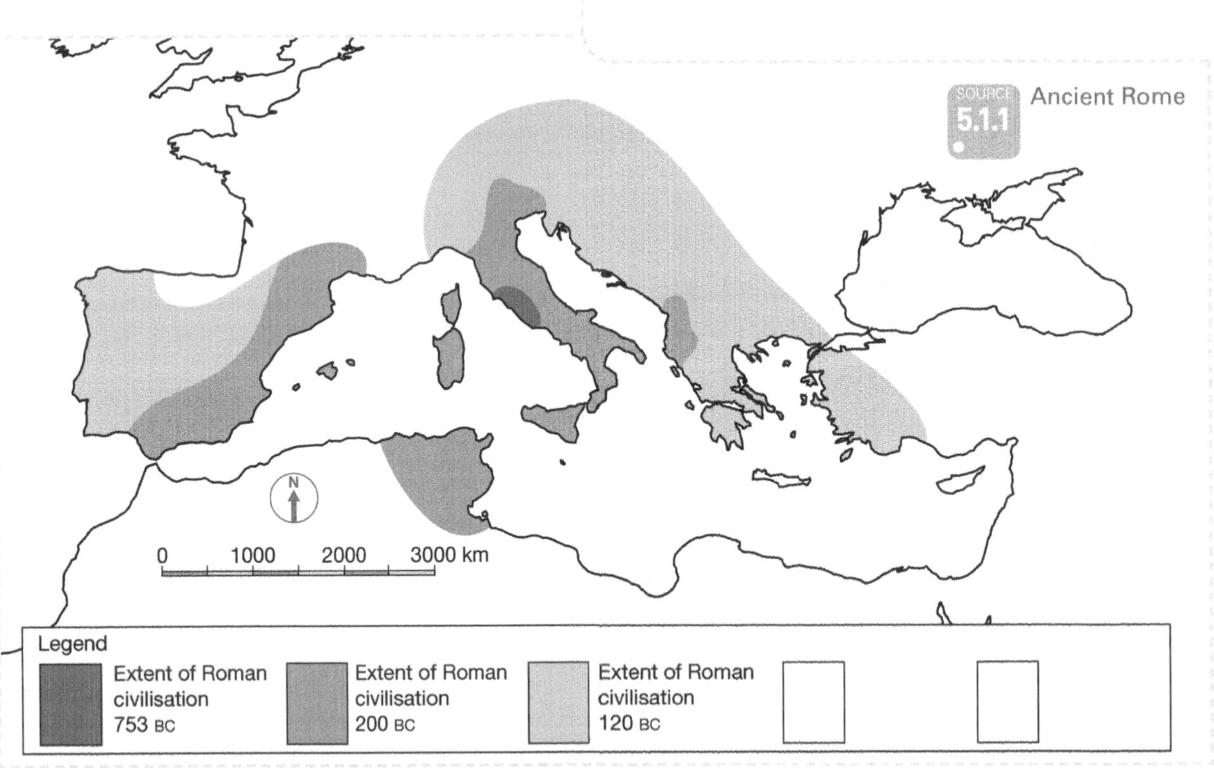

2 Draw a line from east to west across the map, passing through the city of Rome. Use the scale to calculate the width, in kilometres, of the Roman Empire along this line.

____

3 Describe the location of the city of Rome within the Roman Empire.

____

5.2 TIMELINE OF ANCIENT ROME

Key historical events of the Roman civilisation between the years 800 BC and 500 AD are listed below. Place these key events in their correct position on the timeline and label them clearly. It may be helpful to reorganise the list in chronological order first.

146 BC	Rome conquers Greece
264 BC	First Punic War
455 AD	Vandal barbarians attack Rome
509 BC	Roman Republic begins
27 BC	Roman Empire begins
476 AD	Roman Empire ends
753 BC	Romulus and Remus establish Rome
44 BC	Julius Caesar assassinated
70 AD	Building of Colosseum starts
312 BC	Building of Appian Way starts
64 BC	Rome captures Jerusalem
410 AD	Visigoth barbarians attack Rome
79 AD	Pompeii destroyed by eruption of Mount Vesuvius
600 BC	Building of Roman Forum begins
43 AD	Rome invades Britain
570 BC	First census of Roman population

800 BC
700 BC
600 BC
500 BC
400 BC
300 BC
200 BC
100 BC
1 AD
100 AD
200 AD
300 AD
400 AD
500 AD

5.3 LOOKING AT A PRIMARY SOURCE

SOURCE 5.3.1 A Roman carving of the Nile River in Egypt from the second century AD. The carving is held in the Vatican Museums, Vatican City.

1 Look carefully at the Roman carving and answer the following questions.

Label the features on the Roman carving by selecting from the list below. Write your answers in the boxes provided above.

- Nile River
- duck
- hippopotamus
- reeds
- flamingo
- crocodile
- boat
- house

2 Describe the information this Roman carving provides about life along the Nile River in the second century AD.

____

____

____

____

3 Why do you think that the Romans were interested in creating works of art about Egypt? Keep in mind that this is only one example of many pieces of Roman art about Egypt.

____

____

____

____

ROMAN GODS

Gods played an important part in the lives of Ancient Romans. Gods were believed to be responsible for everything that happened on Earth, so people worshipped them in the hope of bringing wealth, health and peace to their lives. The Romans adopted or borrowed their most important gods from the Ancient Greeks but gave them Roman names.

1 Look carefully at the list of the most important Ancient Greek and Roman gods in the following table. Draw a line to match each Roman god with his or her Greek equivalent.

ANCIENT GREEK GOD	ANCIENT ROMAN GOD
Zeus: Chief of all gods; lord of the sky	**Mercury:** Trade, merchants, thieves
Hera: Marriage	**Apollo:** Healing, health, medicine
Athena: Protector of Athens; wise–the owl was her symbol	**Pluto:** The underworld, death
Hermes: Trade, thieves; messenger to the gods	**Ceres:** The Earth, harvest, farming
Demeter: Grain, crops, farming, the harvest	**Venus:** Love, beauty
Apollo: Truth, healing, music	**Mars:** Battles, weapons
Poseidon: Lord of the sea	**Vulcan:** Fire, armour, weapons, volcanoes
Artemis: Hunting	**Minerva:** Wise and talented, her symbol was an owl
Ares: War	**Jupiter:** The greatest god; controlled the sky and weather
Hades: Death; lord of the underworld	**Juno:** Mother, marriage, fertility, childbirth
Aphrodite: Beauty, love	**Diana:** Hunting
Hephaestus: Fire, blacksmiths, weavers, volcanoes	**Bacchus:** Wine
Hestia: The home, hearth, family	**Neptune:** Ships, seafaring
Dionysus: Wine, agriculture	**Vesta:** The home, family, hearth

2 How closely did the Romans copy the Greek gods? Give an example to help explain your answer.

____

____

____

3 Why do you think that Ancient Rome, a powerful civilisation, borrowed gods from the Greeks?

____

____

5.5 LOOKING AT A PRIMARY DOCUMENT

Pliny the Elder was born in 23 AD and died in 79 AD while trying to rescue friends during the eruption of Mount Vesuvius. He was the son of an equestrian who became a navy and army commander. He was also an author. His last work, written in 75 AD, was the *Naturalis Historiae*, an encyclopaedia in which he collected much of the knowledge of his time.

1 Read the following extract and answer the questions.

> In great buildings as well as in other things the rest of the world has been outdone by us Romans. If, indeed, all the buildings in our City are considered … the united grandeur of them would lead one to imagine that we were describing another world, accumulated in a single spot.
>
> Not to mention among our great works the Circus Maximus, that was built by the Dictator Caesar … one *stadium* [about 200 metres] broad and three in length … and occupying with the adjacent buildings no less than four *iugera* [about 10 000 square metres] with room for no less than 160 000 spectators seated …
>
> Frequently praise is given to the great sewer system of Rome. There are seven 'rivers' made to flow, by artificial channels, beneath the city … to carry off and sweep away all the sewage.

SOURCE 5.5.1 From Pliny's *Naturalis Historiae*

2 **a** What is a primary document?

____

____

____

____

b Explain why the extract from Pliny's *Naturalis Historiae* is considered a primary document.

____

____

____

____

c Select and write down any three words or phrases from the extract that demonstrate Pliny's opinion of the city of Rome.

d In your own words, rephrase what Pliny meant about Rome by the phrase 'another world, accumulated in a single spot'.

e Describe any two features of the Circus Maximus.

f Why was praise frequently given to the Roman sewer system?

g Do you think Ancient Rome was a great city? Explain your answer below.

5.6 NUMBERS AND ALPHABET OF ANCIENT ROME

The symbols that were used as numbers in Ancient Rome are listed below.

I = 1	II = 2	III = 3	IV = 4	V = 5
VI = 6	VII = 7	VIII = 8	IX = 9	X = 10
XI = 11	L = 50	C = 100	D = 500	M = 1000

The following table shows how large numbers were created.

MMXI = 2011 (The two Ms are added to make 2000. XI is 11, which is added to 2000 to make 2011.)
XL = 40 (The larger number, L, is written after the smaller number, X. This means X must be subtracted from L. So 10 is subtracted from 50, which makes this number 40.)
LX = 60 (This time the smaller number is written after the larger one, so X is added to L. This gives the number 60.)

1 Express the following Roman numbers in our numbering system.

a MCMXLIV ______

b MDCCXLVIII ______

c XXXIX ______

d DCD ______

2 Add the following numbers and write the answers in Roman numerals.

a V plus VIII = ______

b DC plus L = ______

c XL plus I plus III = ______

3 The Roman alphabet was identical to the English alphabet except there was no *J*, *U*, *W* or *Y*. All writing was in capitals. No punctuation was used.

a Write your full name using the Roman alphabet. If you require Roman letters for *J*, *U*, *W* or *Y*, select the closest-sounding English equivalent. For example, English *J* could be *D*; *U* could be *A* or *OO*; *W* could be *B* or *V*; and *Y* could be *I* or *E*.

______

______

b Write your address (numbers and words) using the Roman alphabet and Roman numbers. Again, choose the closest-sounding English equivalent for *J*, *U*, *W* or *Y*.

______

______

______

______

SPIRAL WORD PUZZLE

Use the clues to complete the spiral word puzzle. Begin each word at the number given in the clue. Follow the spiral shape and the graduated shading of the puzzle to write down the answers.

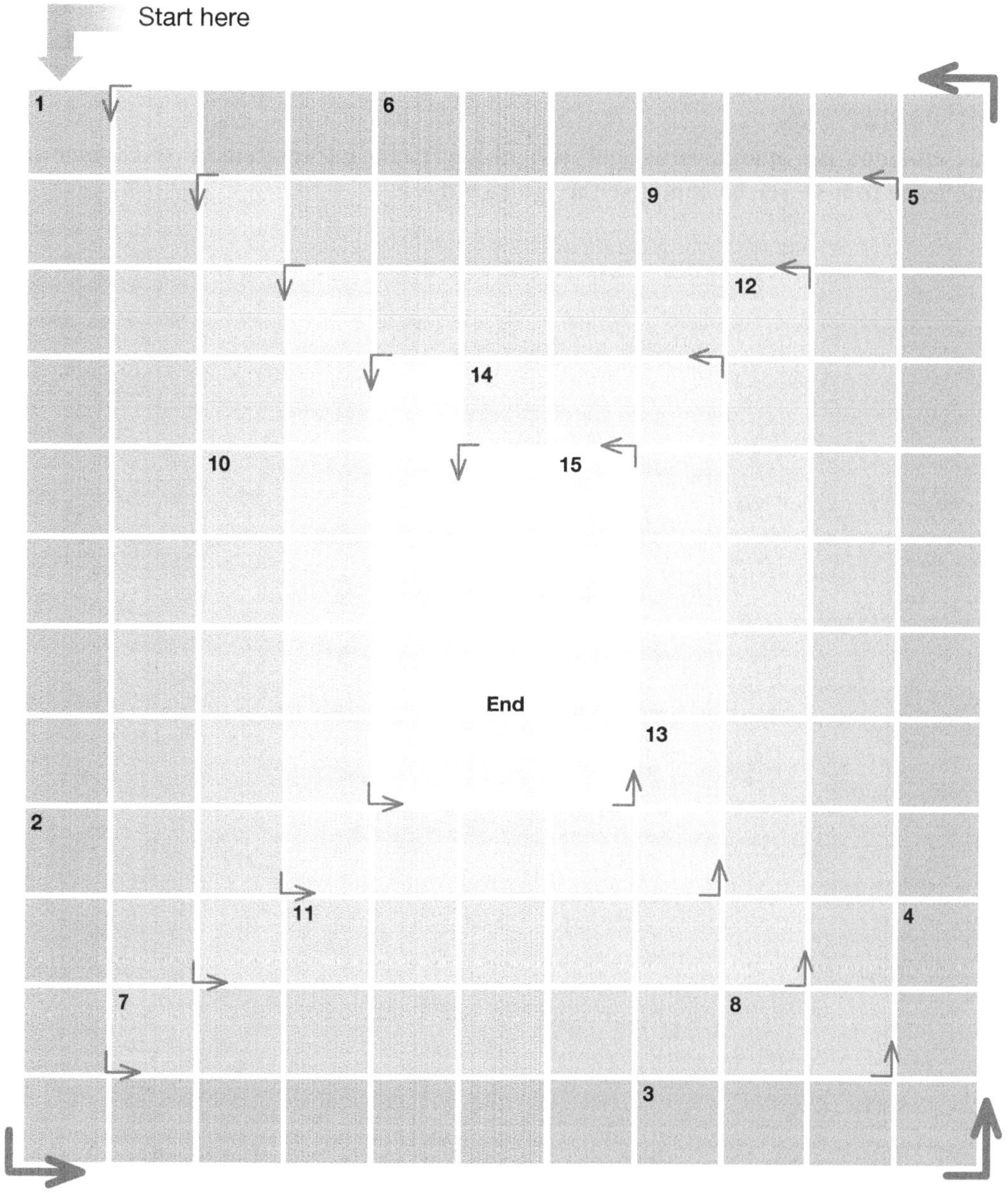

Start here

1 6 9 5 12 14 15 10 End 13 2 11 4 7 8 3

1 earliest period of Roman rule (8 letters)

2 people who fought in the Colosseum and entertained the public (10)

3 river that flows through Rome (5)

4 volcano near present-day Naples that erupted in 79 AD (8)

5 founder of Rome, according to legend (7)

6 location for chariot races in Rome (6–7)

7 Town buried by volcanic eruption (7)

8 Roman leader murdered on the steps of the Senate (6–6)

9 Carthaginian leader during Punic Wars (8)

10 early name given to Rome (6)

11 Roman prisoners were thrown to their deaths from here (8–4)

12 last king of Rome (6–10)

13 title of Roman leaders during the Republic (6)

14 wealthy upper-class citizens (10)

15 abbreviation for Rome's motto *Senatus Populusque Romanus* (4)

5.8 PEOPLE OF ANCIENT ROME

1 The people of Ancient Rome could be grouped into different social classes, with different levels of importance in society. The names of these social groups are the five headings in the table below.

Below the table is a list of words and phrases that describe the social classes. Write each of these words and phrases under the table heading to which it best corresponds. Each word or phrase can only be used once. Some terms are repeated as they apply to more than one class of society.

Conduct research on the internet or in your school library for information on social hierarchy in Ancient Rome to help you to complete the table below.

PATRICIANS	EQUESTRIANS	PLEBEIANS	FOREIGNERS	NON-CITIZENS

- shopkeepers
- governors
- citizens
- free people born outside Rome
- senators
- had no rights as citizens
- had full rights as citizens
- had no rights as citizens
- gained citizenship after 212 BC
- had full rights as citizens
- army officers
- prisoners from conquered territory
- rich businessmen
- builders
- could hold government positions in law
- were sold as property
- wealthy landowners
- citizens
- farmers
- emperors
- could hold government positions in taxation
- slaves
- bakers
- legionaries in army
- were not allowed to vote
- makers of pottery
- had full rights as citizens

2 Use the Venn diagram below to compare and contrast the appearances of Ancient Romans and present-day Australians. Note differences and similarities in clothing, hairstyles and accessories. Conduct research on the internet or in your school library for information on Ancient Rome.

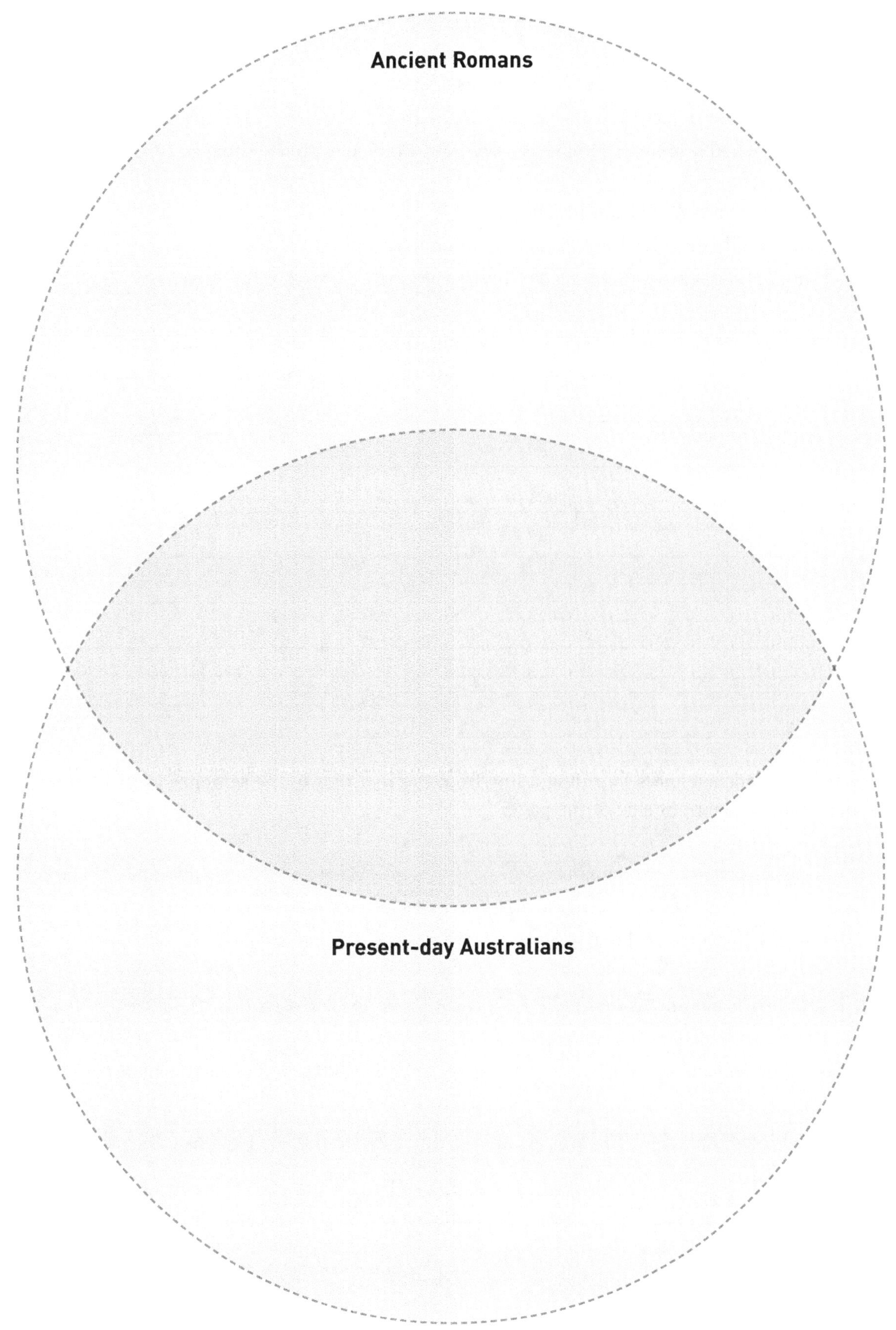

5.9 ROMAN WARFARE

1 Below is a description of some events of the three Punic Wars. The sentences are not in chronological order—that is, they do not correctly show the sequence of events. Rewrite the sentences in the correct order.

Conduct research on the internet or in your school library, for further information on the Punic Wars.

- Rome provoked Carthage until there was a war.
- Hannibal was defeated.
- Carthage had a more experienced navy than Rome but Rome managed to win the war in 241 BC.
- The first Punic War began in 264 BC.
- Rome totally destroyed the Carthaginian civilisation.
- Hannibal, the Carthaginian leader, invaded Rome by crossing the Alps.

2 Match the sentence parts by ruling a line from the first part of the sentence on the left to its ending on the right side of the page.

During the period of the monarchy	plebeians and the wealthy joined the army.
Before the Roman army became professional	smaller than a cohort.
In the professional Roman army	larger than a cohort.
During the Roman Republic	the wealthy joined the Roman army.
Army auxiliaries were filled by	soldiers served full-time.
Army legions were filled by	Roman citizens.
A century of soldiers is	non-citizen volunteers.
A legion of soldiers is	soldiers went home between wars.

3 Roman army battle tactics were carefully planned and executed. The infantry commonly used particular tactics like the tortoise, the wedge, the orb and the skirmishing formation. Select three of these to investigate further. Conduct research into your selected tactics on the internet or in your school library. Use your findings to complete the table.

NAME AND DRAWING OF THE BATTLE TACTIC	DESCRIPTION OF THE BATTLE TACTIC	EXPLANATION OF WHEN THE TACTIC WAS USED

5.10 FAMOUS ROMANS

The Romans created a very powerful civilisation that was very influential across southern Europe, northern Africa and western Asia Minor. Rome's leaders and military personnel played significant roles in establishing and maintaining the empire. Read the information relating to three of these famous people and complete the task that follows.

GAIUS JULIUS CAESAR (100 BC–44 BC)

Julius Caesar was possibly Rome's most famous senator and ruler. Caesar joined the army and began taking an interest in politics as a young man. At twenty years of age he served in the army in Asia. To advance his political career Caesar took lessons in public speaking (oration). By 69 BC Caesar was appointed governor (Quaestor) of Spain. It is said that while in Spain, Caesar saw a statue of Alexander the Great that stirred disappointment in himself, because 'Alexander at my age had conquered so many nations, and I have all this time done nothing that is memorable'.

On his return to Rome, Caesar became a senator and his anti-establishment speeches made him popular with the public. In 60 BC Caesar decided to run for Consul (ruler) and formed a coalition with two wealthy Romans for support; Crassus and Pompey. He won and took office in 59 BC, making his first order a law to make Senate business available to the public. Caesar made many government and social reforms, including the Julian calendar. Between 58 BC and 51 BC Caesar went on military campaigns, the Gallic Wars, which extended Roman territory into central Europe. He was the first Roman to lead an invasion of Britain. Despite his huge public popularity, he was unpopular among conservative senators. A group of senators, led by Marcus Junius Brutus assassinated Caesar in 44 BC.

MARCUS ANTONIUS (83 BC–30 BC)

In English he is more commonly called Mark Antony. His mother was Julius Caesar's cousin and he was a loyal supporter of Caesar. He became a Roman politician and military general. In 57 BC Antony took part in successful military campaigns in central Europe, the Gallic Wars. Antony commanded Italy while Caesar invaded Spain and Greece. His support of Caesar led to Antony's temporary expulsion from the senate. Caesar appointed him administrator of Rome in 47 BC but removed him from the position soon after when Antony's extravagant lifestyle and poor administration resulted in violence, deaths and disorder.

Antony and Caesar remained friends. Antony gave the eulogy at Caesar's funeral. This inspired the sixteenth century English playwright William Shakespeare's famous speech beginning, 'Friends, Romans, countrymen, lend me your ears'. He named and accused the murderers and dramatically removed Caesar's cloak to reveal the stab wounds. The Roman public was stirred into taking action, attacking the assassins' houses that night and forcing them to flee.

Antony is well known for his relationship with Cleopatra, the last pharaoh of Egypt. They lived together in Egypt. Antony's Roman enemies declared war on Antony. Believing that Antony died in battle, Cleopatra killed herself. On hearing of her death, Antony killed himself.

NERO CLAUDIUS CAESAR AUGUSTUS GERMANICUS (37 AD–68 AD)

Known more commonly as Nero, this infamous Roman was the fifth emperor of the Roman Empire. Nero became ruler in 54 AD. At first, Nero concentrated on diplomacy, trade and improving the cultural life of Rome. He supported athletic games and ordered theatres to be built. In 64 AD Nero was blamed for starting the Great Fire of Rome. It was said that Nero played the fiddle while Rome burned, though this is not historically accurate. Later he used the burnt land to build the Domus Aurea (Golden House).

The villa was enormous and luxurious; man-made lakes, 300 rooms, gold leaf and precious stone decorations, mosaic floors, surrounding fields with orchards and flocks of animals.

Nero is remembered as an extravagant Emperor and a tyrant. He order many executions, including that of his mother and is suspected of arranging the murder of his stepbrother. He persecuted Christians. There were rumours that captured Christians were burnt in his garden at night as a source of light.

In 68 AD, some of Nero's governors rebelled against his taxation policies. Support for the rebels increased. Nero attempted to flee Rome but his army officers refused to obey him. He returned to Rome and heard that the Senate had declared him a public enemy. Rather than be executed by being beaten to death, he took his own life.

Read the statements below. Decide which famous Roman each statement most likely relates to. Indicate your answer by writing the famous Roman's name in the space provided.

STATEMENT	FAMOUS ROMAN'S NAME
I had a luxurious villa built in Rome.	
I was 53 years old when I died.	
Only I know what I did while Rome burned.	
When a young man, I served in the army in Asia.	
I am related to Julius Caesar.	
I made government more transparent by allowing the public to know what happens in the Senate.	
I am very ambitious but feel the achievements of Alexander the Great dwarf my own.	
I killed myself when I learnt that my lover, the pharaoh of Egypt, had died.	
I enjoyed total power, using it to rid the Empire of Christians.	
William Shakespeare was inspired by my speech to write, 'Friends, Romans, countrymen ...'	
My opponents in politics assassinated me because they disagreed with my progressive ideas.	
Crassus and Pompey support me in my efforts to become ruler of Rome.	
My army turned against me and refused to help me escape from Rome.	
I fought in the Gallic wars, along with Caesar.	
On my order, my mother was executed.	
Brutus and a group of other senators are my assassins.	
During my reign my focus is to improve the cultural life of Rome.	
I am a failure in administration, allowing Rome to become lawless under my control.	
I am the first Roman ruler to invade Britain.	

LEGACIES OF ANCIENT ROME

1 Read the passage below and complete it by writing the correct word or words from the list below in each of the spaces. Add a capital letter if you need to.

Ancient Rome was technically advanced for its time. ______________________ led the ancient world in a wide variety of fields. The ______________________ were the first written laws, and they led to a fairer and more consistent ______________________. Romans also developed a system of evaluating a person's innocence or guilt in relation to a crime. The accused person had a ______________________ judged by a jury.

Romans were excellent engineers. Many of their roads, ______________________ and sewers still exist today. A famous Roman road was the ______________________.

Long ______________________ transported water to towns and cities. ______________________ or latrines were built, as well as ______________________, in order to maintain cleanliness and improve hygiene.

The Romans invented a ______________________ for buildings, called a hypocaust, to make the cold winters more comfortable. ______________________ Roman buildings could be constructed because of the invention of ______________________. Modern ______________________ still use many ideas and technologies handed down from Ancient Rome. Although thousands of years have passed, we still look to the Ancient Romans and benefit from the ______________________ they left us.

- Twelve Tables
- toilets
- public baths
- bridges
- Appian Way
- legal system
- heating system
- Rome
- trial
- societies
- legacies
- multistorey
- concrete
- aqueducts

2 Triangle A is divided into nine smaller triangles. Each side of the smaller triangles has a clue written on it. The smaller triangles are arranged so that none of the clues match each other.

Triangle B is also divided into nine smaller triangles. Triangle B has clues written around the outside.

a Using tracing paper, carefully copy the nine small triangles in Triangle A, making sure you include the clues.

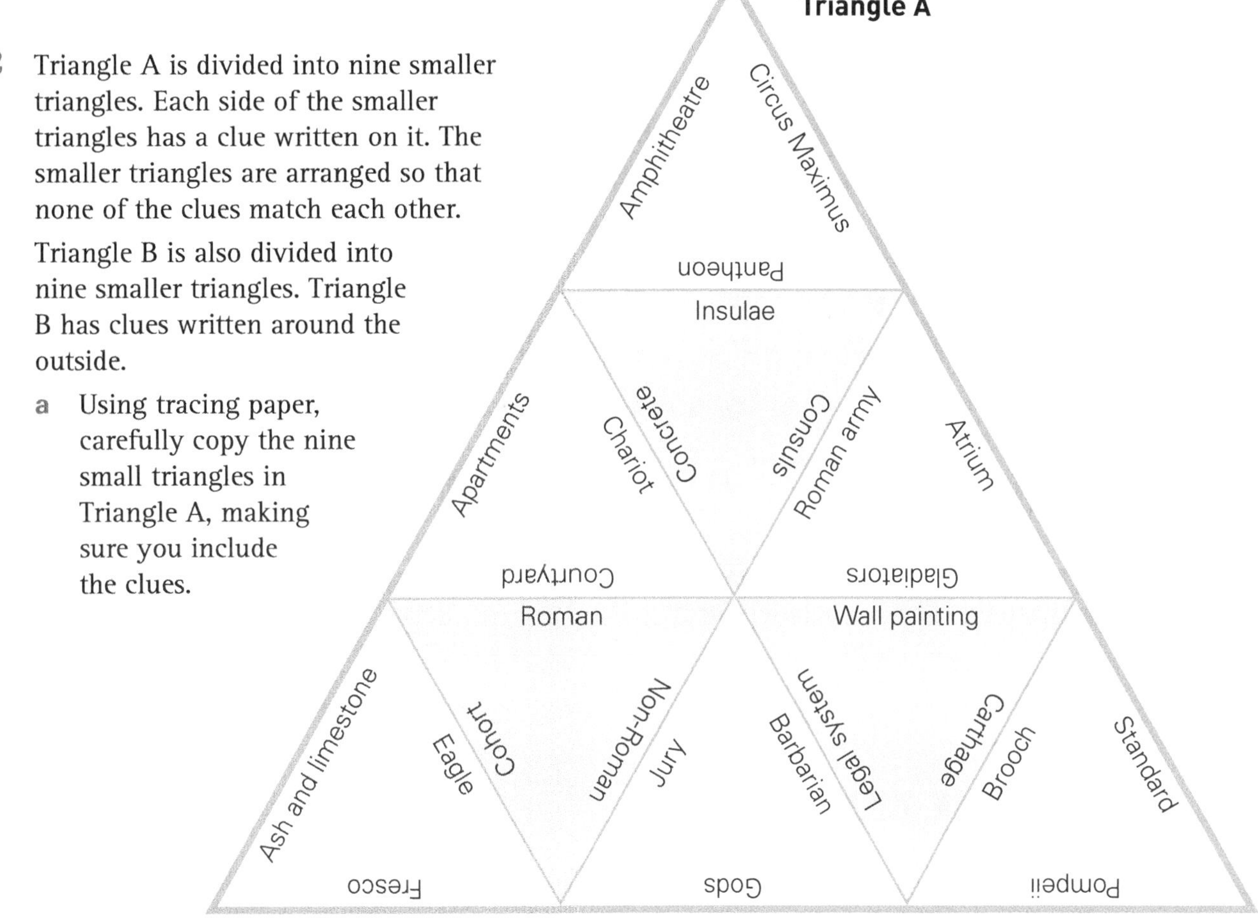

b Cut out the nine small triangles.

c Place the nine small traced triangles onto Triangle B so that all the clues match each other on all sides. The clues on the outer edges of the small triangles should also match the clues on the outside of Triangle B.

d Once you are sure the small triangles are positioned correctly, paste them in place.

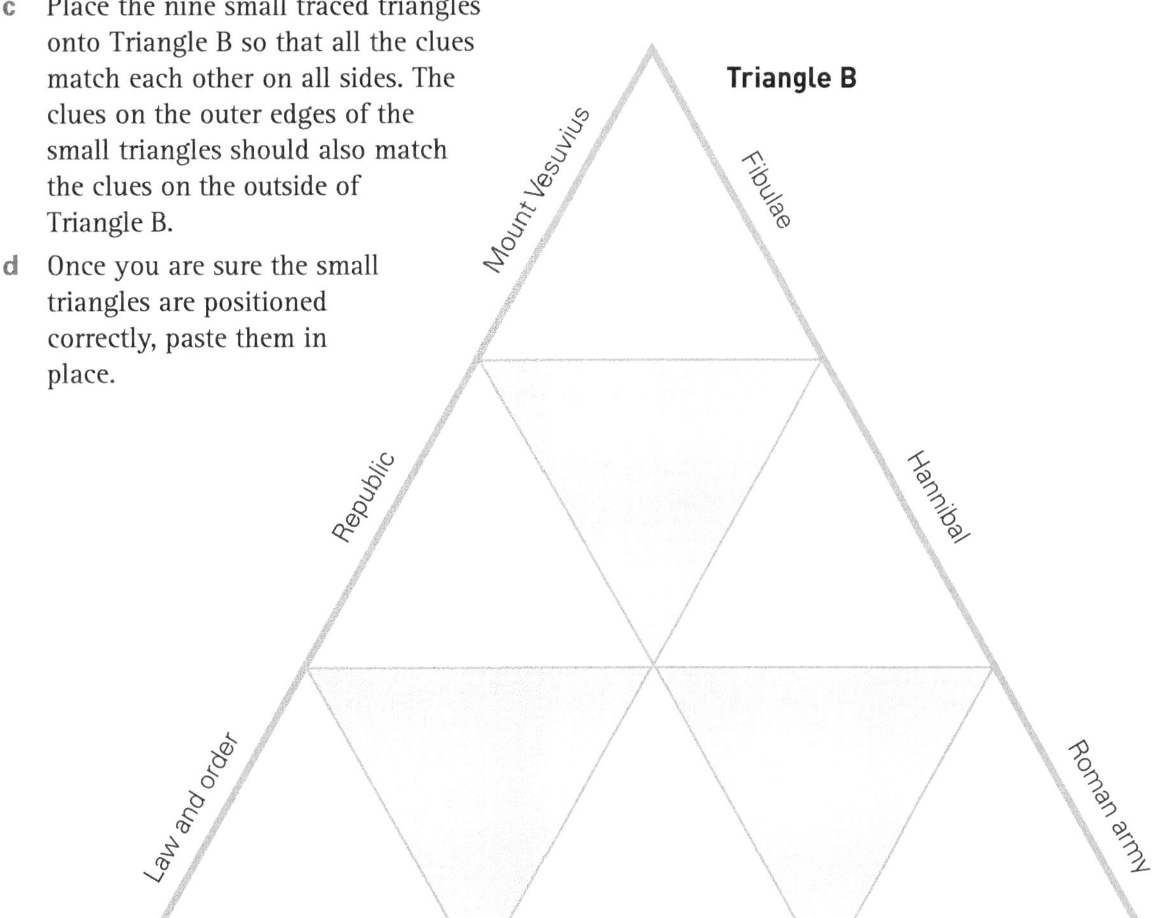

CHAPTER 6: ANCIENT INDIA

TIMELINE OF ANCIENT INDIA

The timeline shows the development of two tribal groups, the Dravidians and Aryans, which together make up India's population today.

SOURCE 6.1.1 Ancient India timeline

Date	Dravidians	Aryans
4000 BC	First human settlement in Indus Valley	Settle in eastern Europe and Iran
2600 BC	Peak of Indus Valley civilisation	
2000 BC	Indus Valley civilisations start to decline	
1600 BC		Aryans move into India in Indus Valley
1000 BC	Vedic culture starts in India	
900 BC		Aryans move to Ganges Valley. Aryans now called Indo-Aryans
321–184 BC	Mauryan Empire	
320–415 AD	Gupta Empire	

1 Look at the timeline and complete the following questions. Conduct research on Ancient India, on the internet or in your school library to help you.

a In 4000 BC, where did the Dravidians and Aryans have their settlements?

____

____

b What might have attracted settlers to the Indus Valley?

____

____

c Which tribe first settled the subcontinent (southern Asia around India)?

____

2 Explain why historians refer to the group of people as the 'Aryans' earlier in India's history and 'Indo-Aryans' later in time. Are these two different groups of people? Explain your answer.

____

____

____

____

6.2 MAP OF ANCIENT INDIA

Look carefully at the map of southern Asia, including India, to help you complete the following questions.

SOURCE 6.2.1 Ancient India

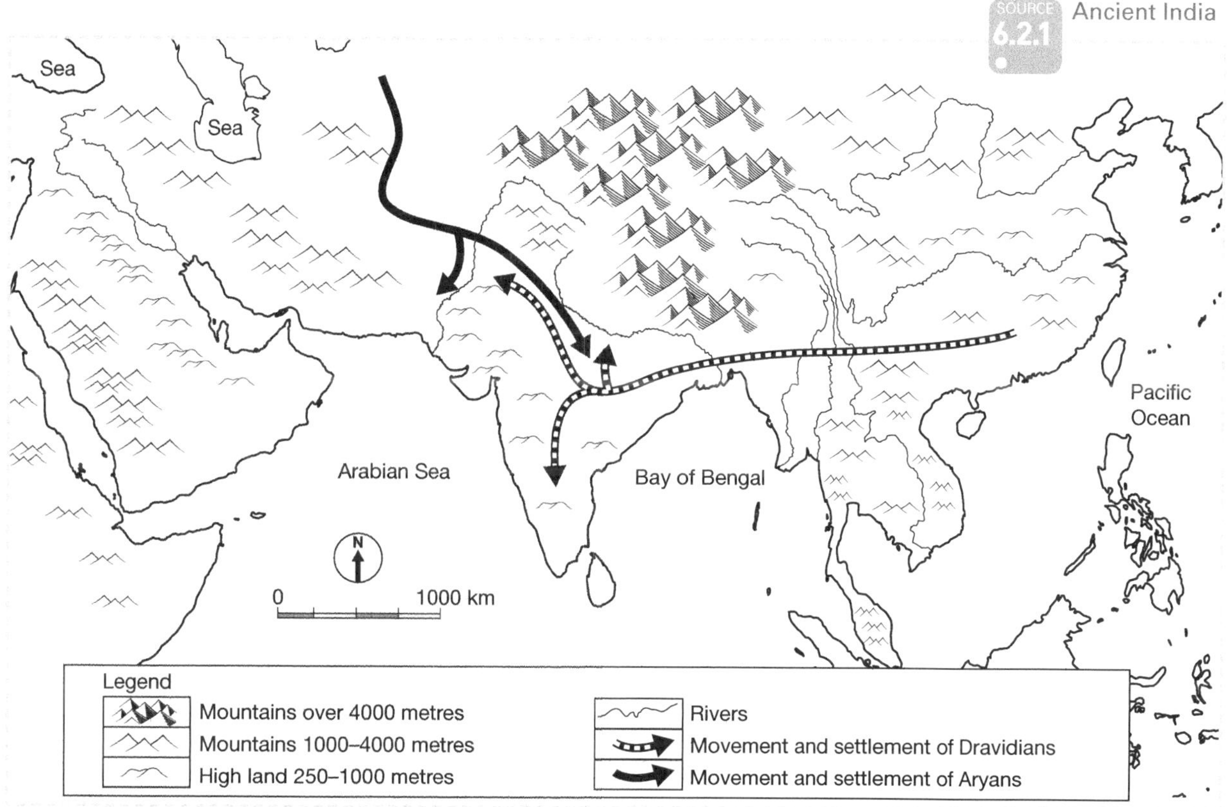

1 Label the Indus and Ganges rivers on the map.

2 Where did the Dravidians migrate from to come to India?

____

3 Where did the Aryans settle once they moved into India?

____

4 What physical barriers would have influenced migration routes of tribes of people across Asia?

____

____

5 Use a green coloured pencil to show where you think the most densely populated parts of Ancient India would have been. Explain why you selected these areas.

____

____

6 Identify two other areas on the map where the conditions were suitable to attract settlements. Colour these two areas in red and explain why you think these areas could attract settlements.

____

____

____

6.3 AN EPIC CARTOON

An epic is a long series of events. This cartoon tells the tale of the Ancient Indian epic, The *Ramayana.*

Look at the cartoon then answer the questions about this famous story. You may find it useful to conduct research on the *Ramayana* on the internet or in your school library.

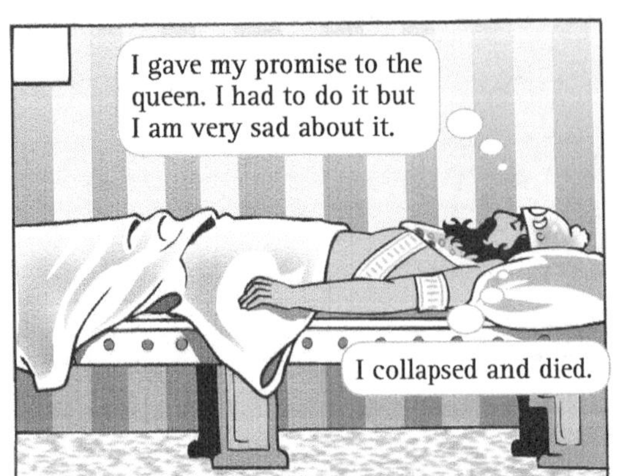

1 The cartoon pictures are out of order. Sort the pictures into their correct order. Do this by numbering them from 1 to 8 in the space provided in the top left corner of each picture.

2 Identify the main characters in each cartoon frame and mark them in different colours.

PICTURE NUMBER	CHARACTER NAME	COLOUR

3 When was this epic written?

4 Rewrite this story in your own words.

6.4 PRIMARY SOURCES

BUDDHISM

Siddhartha Gautama was the founder of Buddhism. He left his life as a prince to wander the countryside as a beggar, seeking understanding and happiness. He became known as Buddha, meaning 'enlightened one'. His teachings included eight rules for leading a good life, attaining perfection and finding a state of peace called nirvana.

Two extracts from Buddha's teachings are written below. Read them carefully and answer the questions that follow.

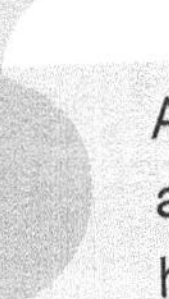

> All that we are is the result of what we have thought. If a person speaks or acts with an evil thought, pain follows. If a person speaks or acts kindly, happiness follows.

SOURCE 6.4.1 This extract is from *The Dhammapada*, a book of verses uttered by the Buddha on various occasions.

> If a man does me wrong, I will return to him my ungrudging love. The more evil that comes from him the more good shall come from me.

SOURCE 6.4.2 This extract, also from *The Dhammapada*, gives advice about what to do if someone treats you poorly.

1 According to Buddha, what is the consequence of thinking evil thoughts?

____

____

____

2 How is happiness achieved?

____

____

____

3 How should Buddhists behave towards people who harm them?

____

____

____

4 Why should a person do good deeds?

____

____

____

HERO STONES

Hero stones are carved memorial stones that honour the death of a hero. The hero might have died in battle or defending his village against thieves or attackers. The hero stone shows scenes of the events that led to the death. When a male hero died, his wife would sometimes throw herself on the husband's funeral fire and die with him. This custom was called 'sati' or 'suttee' and was highly regarded. It was evidence of a virtuous wife, who, it was believed, went straight to heaven. The deaths of the husband and wife were honoured on sati stones. These stones had carvings of both the hero and his wife.

Look carefully at the image below to answer the questions.

5 Does this monument appear to be a hero stone or sati stone? Why?

____

____

6 Look at the top panel of carving. Which figure appears to be the hero? Why?

____

____

____

7 What seems to be happening in the middle panel?

____

____

____

SOURCE 6.4.3 Hero stone in the grounds of the State Archaeological Museum, Bangalore, Karnataka, India

8 Which figure seems to be the hero in the lowest panel? Give two reasons to support your answer.

____

____

____

____

____

9 What do you think happened to make a hero of the person for whom this hero stone was carved?

____

____

____

____

____

VOLUMES OF VEDAS

The Vedas were religious texts that guided Indian culture from 2000 BC. They were passed from generation to generation by word of mouth but by 600 BC they were recorded in writing.

Veda means 'gaining knowledge for enlightenment and spiritual happiness'. The knowledge of the Vedas was about creation and the creator of all things. There are three groups of Vedas:

- those that comprise *Rig Veda*, *Sama Veda* and *Yajar Atharva*
- Brahmanas
- Vedanta Upanishads.

Indicate whether the following statements about Ancient India are true or false. Conduct research on the Vedas on the internet or in your school library to help you.

	TRUE OR FALSE?
The Vedas are archaeological records of India's Neolithic history.	
The Vedas were written in the ancient Sanskrit language.	
The oldest Veda is the *Atharva Veda.*	
The Brahmanas were written after the Vedanta Upanishads.	
The Vedas were written as poetry.	
The Brahmanas are comments on the Vedas.	
Gurus wrote the Vedanta Upanishads to question the power of the priests.	
The Vedas were writings of the Dravidian people.	
The Vedas are religious writings.	
The *Rig Veda* consists of 1000 poems.	
The Vedas led to the Hindu religion.	
The Vedas were written at the same time as society was divided into a strict caste system.	

6.6 A PLACE IN THE WORLD

Ancient Hindu identifies four varnas or social classes. Some believe that the importance and order of different social groups is related to the god Brahma and the part of his body from which they were created.

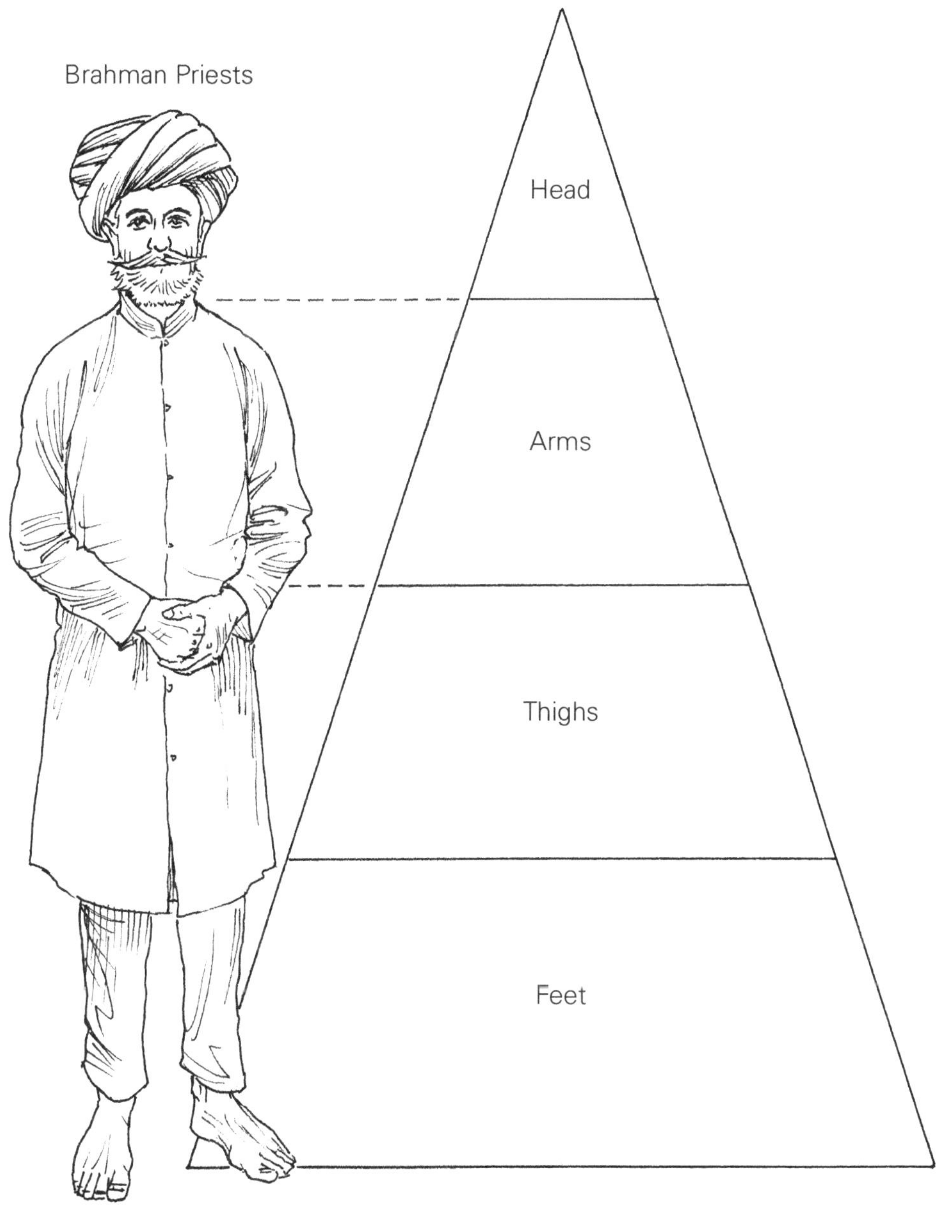

1 The pyramid representing India's social classes is partly filled in. Fill in the rest of the pyramid by writing in the names of the social groups. Conduct research on social classes in Ancient India, on the internet or in your school library to help you.

2 Write the following jobs in the correct social classes on the pyramid:

- servant
- farmer
- warrior
- merchant
- labourer
- ruler
- craftsman.

3 There was an even lower caste than those on the pyramid. What was it called? What jobs did people of this caste do?

____

____

____

6.7 PRIMARY SOURCES: THE INDUS VALLEY

The Indus Valley was the location of India's earliest civilisation. Two major cities grew there; Harappa and Mohenjo-Daro. The cities were well established by 2600 BC. Both cities were citadels, meaning they were fortress cities with protective walls.

1 Conduct some research on the internet or in your school library. Locate the Indus Valley and the ancient cities of Harappa and Mohenjo-Daro. Mark the sites of the two cities on source 6.7.1.

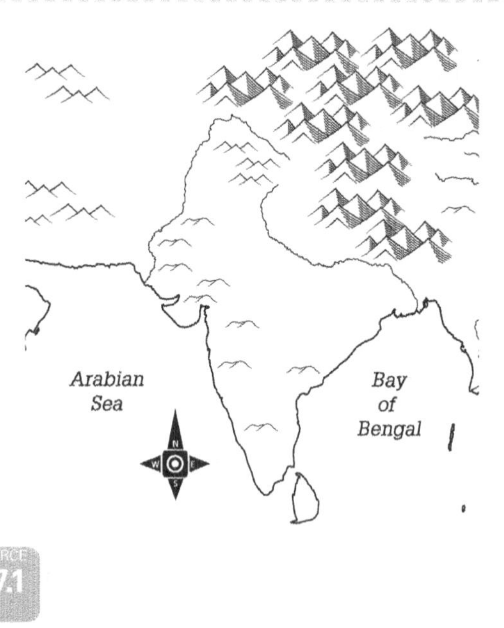

SOURCE 6.7.1

SOURCE 6.7.2 A ceramic object from Mohenjo-Daro.

SOURCE 6.7.3 The ruins of Mohenjo-Daro. The site is now protected as a UNESCO World Heritage Site.

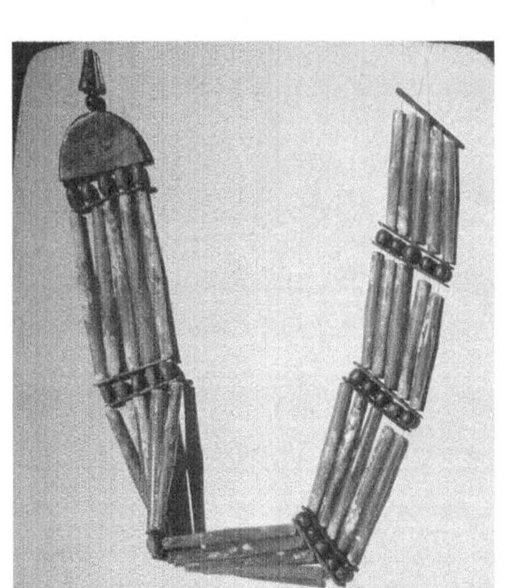

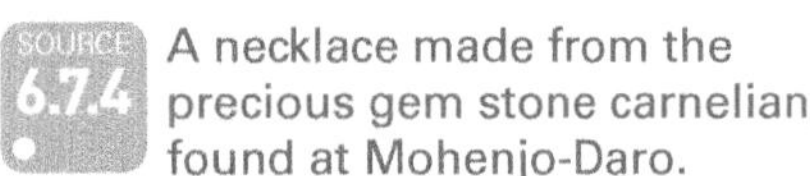

SOURCE 6.7.4 A necklace made from the precious gem stone carnelian, found at Mohenjo-Daro.

SOURCE 6.7.5 A seal from Mohenjo-Daro carved on the soft mineral, talc. Archeologists have found many similar seals.

SOURCE 6.7.6 The remains of the Harappa granaries, the storage places for threshed grains.

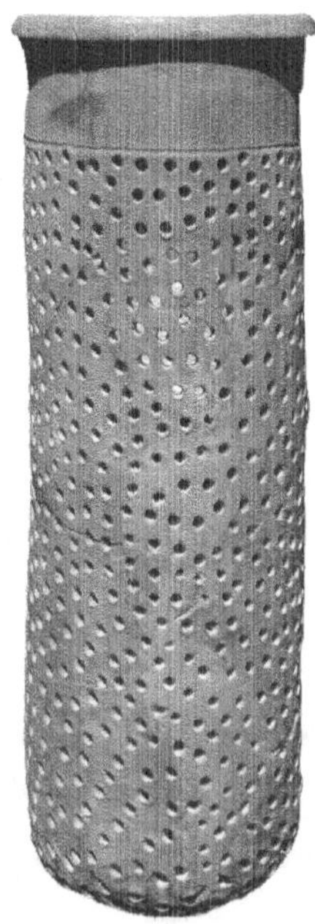

SOURCE 6.7.7 A ceramic pot dotted with holes from Harappa.

2 Look carefully at sources 6.7.2 to 6.7.7 of the sites and artefacts from Harappa and Mohenjo-Daro. Use evidence from the sources to complete the graphic organiser below, showing your conclusions about occupations, technology/crafts, communication, and buildings/town planning. State the source from which you drew each conclusion.

Occupations

Technology/Crafts

The Indus Valley civilisation:
Harappa and Mohenjo-Daro

Communication

Buildings/Town planning

6.8 THE AJANTA CAVES

It is estimated that there are over 1500 rock cut architectural caves in India. The Ajanta Caves are amongst these. It is typical of these caves to be perched on cliff faces with caves dug into hard basalt or granite rocks. The Ajanta Caves in the Maharashtra district contain the oldest and best Indian rock paintings from the second century BC. They are Buddhist shrines that served as an important religious centre. in central India. The caves were given UNESCO World Heritage status in 1983. The caves are symbols of the golden age of Indian culture.

The caves were abandoned about 480 AD when Buddhist monasteries lost support with the end of the Vakataka Empire. Dense jungle grew and concealed the caves. They were accidently discovered in 1819 by John Smith, a British army officer who entered the gorge of the Waghora River while hunting tigers.

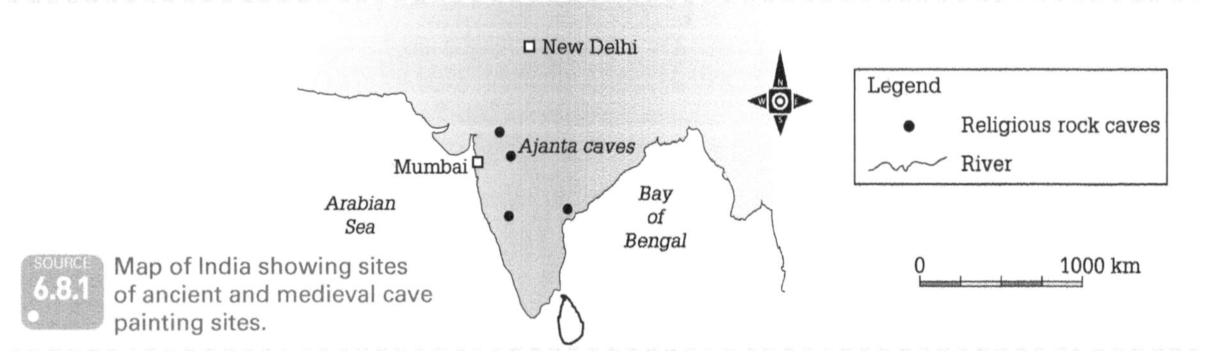

SOURCE 6.8.1 Map of India showing sites of ancient and medieval cave painting sites.

1 Describe the distribution of religious rock caves in India.

---

2 Devotees of which religion built the caves?

---

3 **a** For how many years were the caves abandoned before they were discovered by Captain Smith?

---

b Imagine you were Captain Smith, who discovered the caves after they had been abandoned for so long. Complete the Y-chart below, to describe what you saw, what you heard and what you felt upon making the discovery.

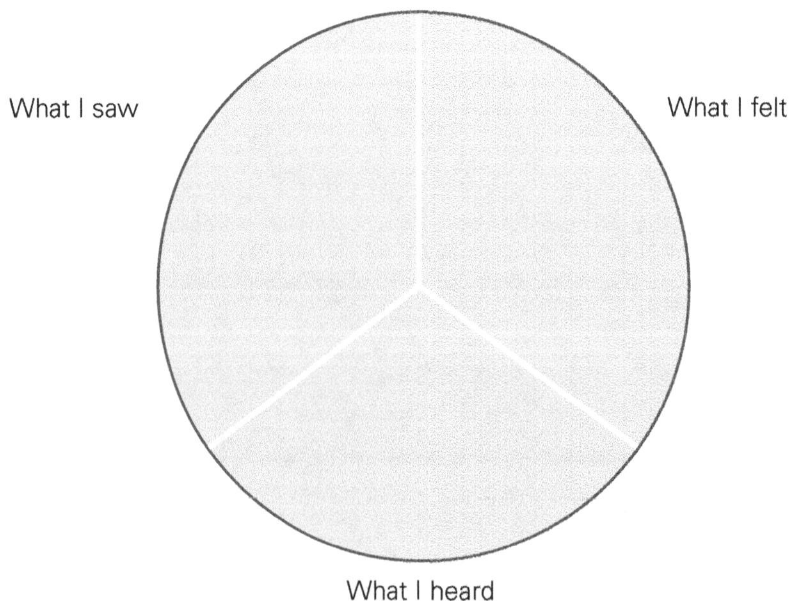

CAVE 1

- A monastery for prayer and living
- Best preserved cave
- Cave entrance has elaborate carvings of the life of Buddha
- Main hall is six metres high
- A shrine at the rear with a seated Buddha
- Dormitory rooms surround main hall

CAVE 6

- A monastery
- A two story structure

CAVE 10

- A sanctuary
- This was the cave discovered by Captain Smith

CAVE 16

- A monastery
- Beautiful paintings
- Two elephant statues next to stairway
- Inscription that the prime minister was a patron (gave funds) for its creation

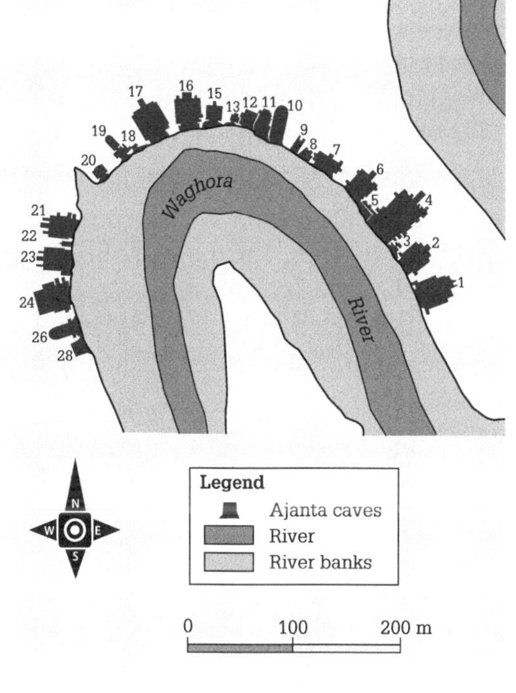

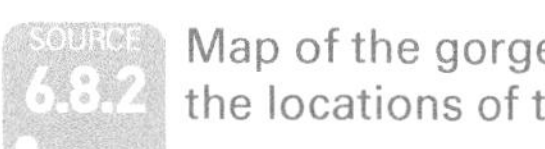
SOURCE 6.8.2 Map of the gorge showing the locations of the caves

SOURCE 6.8.3 Interior of Ajanta Cave number 19

SOURCE 6.8.4 Access to the caves is now along a path constructed along the cliff. Originally access to each cave was obtained by a staircase from the river below.

4 Refer to source 6.8.2 and identify two similarities and two differences between the caves.

____

____

____

____

____

BUDDHA: RICHES TO RAGS

Religion is one of ancient India's influences on the modern world. Two of the world's great religions originated in India: Buddhism and Hinduism. Today, there are around 1 billion Hindus, making up over thirteen per cent of the total world population and about 376 million Buddhists, accounting for almost seven per cent of the world population.

The principle of non-violence towards living things, called ahimsa, comes from the Buddhist and Hindu religions. The Indian political leader Gandhi used ahimsa in the mid-twentieth century to fight the British colonists and gain independence for India. In the United States of America in the 1960s, the civil rights leader Martin Luther King Jr. was influenced by Indian religions to organise peaceful protests against inequality for African-Americans.

1 One very important figure in the growth of religious ideals in ancient India was Buddha. Read the story of the life of Buddha. Complete the story by writing in the correct word from the list provided.

- Buddhism
- shocked
- Hinduism
- prophets
- society
- Nepalese-Indian
- teaching
- palace
- convert
- suffering
- clothes
- India
- persuaded
- poisoning
- Siddhartha

Siddhartha Gautama was born in 563 BC near the ____________________ border. His father was king of the Sakya tribe. The king named his son ____________________ meaning 'a person of success and prosperity'. Even as a baby, ____________________ said he had supreme knowledge and would become either a world political or religious leader.

Siddhartha led a privileged life in the ____________________, sheltered from the realities of outside world. At the age of sixteen he married Princess Yasodhara. One day in 533 BC he ____________________ a groom to take him to the nearby town where he had never before been. This trip and three that followed left him ____________________. He saw things he did not know existed: old age, suffering, death, sickness and poverty. These sights changed his life forever. In the same year he secretly escaped from the palace and began his travels across ____________________.

Siddhartha began a spiritual life. He shaved his head, replaced his princely ____________________ with common robes and became a student of Brahman (superior Hindu caste) teachers. For five years, from 533 BC he searched for enlightenment. Instead, he grew to dislike the rigid caste system of ____________________ and became disillusioned with Hinduism. Buddha abandoned ____________________. Instead he tried to reach truth through meditation.

In 528 BC, while meditating under a tree, he experienced the Great Enlightenment. The way to salvation was through ____________________. This understanding became the basis of ____________________. Buddha made his first sermon to his disciples. In 527 BC he returned to the palace briefly to ______________________ the royal family. The rest of his life was spent travelling across northern India, ______________________ and converting tens of thousands of people from all walks of life, to Buddhism. Buddha died in 483 BC at 80 years of age, of food ______________________. His last words were 'All compounded things are ephemeral; work diligently on your salvation'.

2 Reread the story of the life of Buddha. Use key events and dates to create a timeline of Buddha's life.

3 Reread the last words uttered by Buddha. With the help of a dictionary, rewrite the statement in your own words.

____

____

____

____

4 What does Buddha's life tell you about how Buddhists should lead their lives?

____

____

____

____

5 What do you think might have happened if the king had not confined and isolated Siddhartha in the palace for the first thirty years of his life? Explain the reasons for your answer.

____

____

____

____

____

____

____

CHAPTER 7: ANCIENT CHINA

TIMELINE OF ANCIENT CHINA

Sort the events that occurred in Ancient China into the specific period in which they happened–Neolithic China, or the dynasties of Xia, Shang, Zhou, Qin or Han, then write the events on the timeline. Conduct research on the internet or in your school library to help you.

EVENTS OF ANCIENT CHINA

- Great Wall built
- Human sacrifice banned
- Feudal system developed
- Artefacts found at Erlitou
- First emperor
- Tribes located around Yangshao and Lungshan
- Primitive agriculture used
- Chinese writing invented
- Terracotta Army made
- Earliest bronze vessels made
- Philosophers flourish
- 30 kings during this period
- Hunt and gather food
- Bureaucracy replaces feudal system
- Confucianism is main philosophy
- Considered a mythical time until evidence proves otherwise
- Earliest iron tools
- Oracle bones discovered
- Trade along Silk Road

Neolithic 18 000–2000 BC

2000 BC

Xia dynasty 2000–1766 BC

Shang dynasty 1766–1027 BC

1000 BC

Zhou dynasty 1122–481 BC

Western Zhou

Eastern Zhou

Spring and autumn

Warring States

Qin dynasty 221–207 BC

1 AD

Han dynasty 202 BC – 220 AD

1000 AD

7.2 THE EARLY DYNASTIES

Ancient China's earliest dynasty formed around 2205 BC. Between that date and 481 BC three dynasties ruled China; the Xia, Shang and Zhou dynasties.

Conduct some research into these dynasties on the internet or in your school library to help you complete the following information about ancient China's three early dynasties. Fill in the gaps by using the correct terms provided below.

- primary
- Xia
- dynasty
- cemetery
- Shang
- bones
- fire
- valleys
- disobey
- philosophers
- secondary
- bronze
- cracks
- archaeologists
- king
- authority

The earliest dynasties formed along the ____________________ of the Yellow and Yangzi Rivers. The strongest warlord became ____________________. Evidence of the existence of the ____________________ Dynasty was not uncovered for thousands of years after the ____________________ ended. Ancient Chinese texts gave accounts of that period. These texts however, were ____________________ documents, written after the dynasty ended. Archeologists did not find the ____________________ evidence until 1959 when they unearthed the ruins of an old city at Erlitou.

Like the Xia Dynasty, primary evidence of the existence of the ____________________ Dynasty (1766 BC to 1122 BC) was found in the twentieth century. In 1930 ____________________ discovered the ancient city of Shang and its royal ____________________. Amongst the artifacts discovered were many ____________________ items like alcohol containers, axe blades and weapons. A curious discovery was many shells and cattle ____________________ that had inscriptions scratched into them. These oracle bones were used to tell the future. Fortune-tellers scratched questions on the bones. The bones were placed in a ____________________. From the ____________________ that appeared on the heated bones, fortune-tellers would tell the future.

The Zhou Dynasty ruled China from 1122 BC to 481 BC. This dynasty was a time of great ____________________ and advances in technology. Confucius developed his ideas about how to be a good person. The ____________________ of the kings grew. They claimed to be chosen from heaven to be rulers or to have a 'mandate from Heaven'. To disobey the king was to ____________________ Heaven.

7.3 MAP OF ANCIENT CHINA

The map shows the present and ancient past territories and borders of China. Please note that some dynasties have been grouped together to simplify the map. Look carefully at the map and conduct research on the internet and in your school library. Answer the questions that follow.

SOURCE 7.3.1 Ancient China

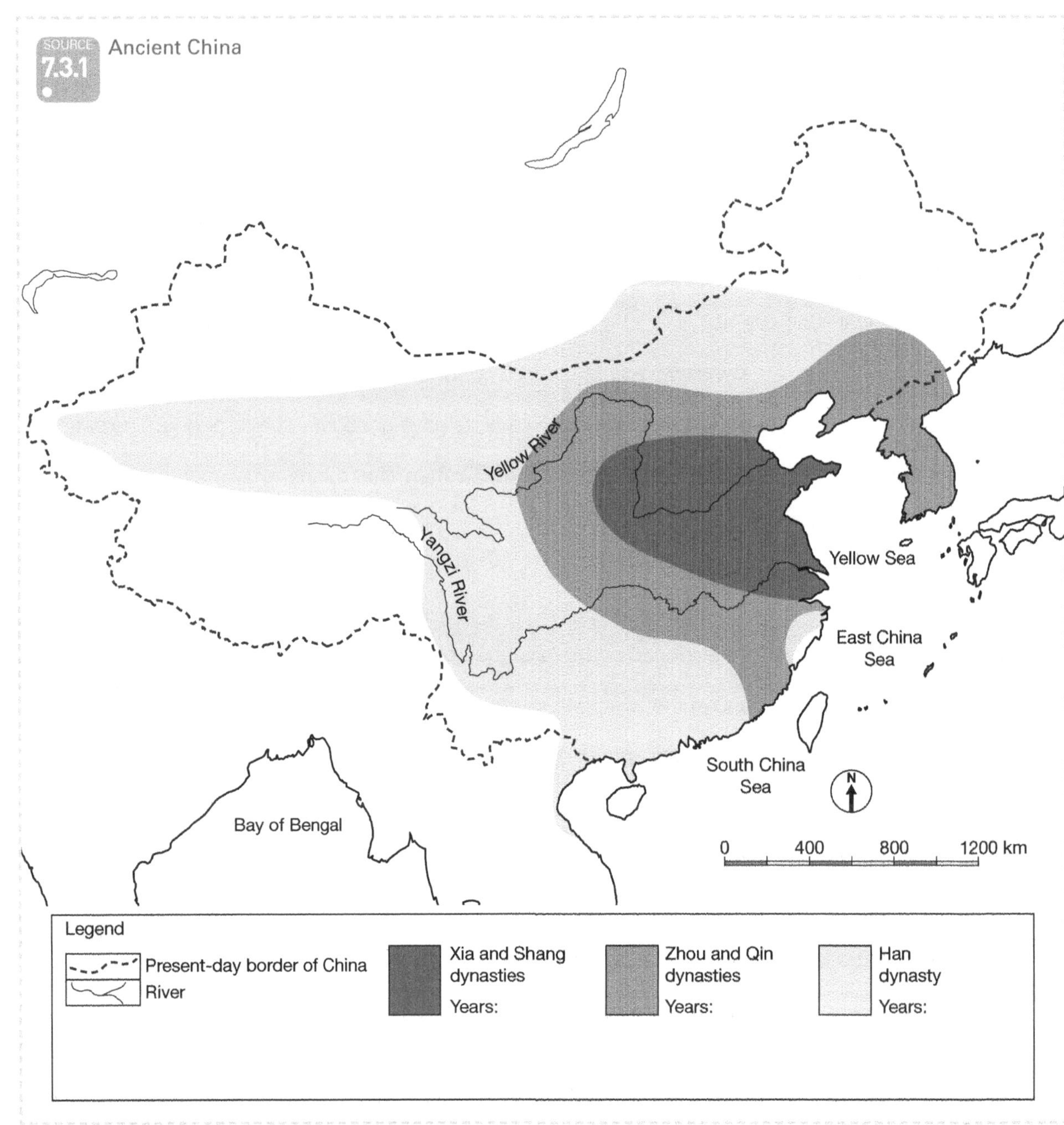

1 The legend for the map includes shading for Chinese territory during the ancient dynasties. Some dynasties are represented together as one colour. In the space below the names of the dynasties, write the beginning and end dates of the groups of dynasties shown.

2 Where and when did the earliest Chinese settlements begin?

3 Which dynasty or group of dynasties had the largest territory?

4 Between the end of the Han dynasty and the present day, China lost some territory and gained other territory. Use red to shade all the territory China gained in this period. Use blue to show the territory lost. Compare the difference in size of Ancient and modern China.

5 How can you explain the extension of Chinese settlement to the west of China during the Han dynasty?

6 During what dynasty did building of the Great Wall begin? Would it have been an effective barrier to protect China at that time?

7 Outline whether the Great Wall was an effective barrier against the 'barbarians' during the Han dynasty.

8 What was the widest extent of Ancient China, measuring from east to west? Begin measuring from the mouth of the Yellow River.

9 What influence, if any, did China's two main rivers have on the spread of settlement during ancient times? Explain your answer.

7.4 PRIMARY SOURCES

THE POTTERY HOUSE

Ancient Chinese burial sites were filled with possessions for use in the next life. The rich had particularly beautiful tombs with many decorations and a wide array of belongings. Before the Qin dynasty, animals and servants were also buried with the king so he could be looked after in the next life. In later periods pottery models of people and animals were buried with the king instead of living things.

The pottery model of a farm house, shown below, was discovered by archaeologists in a tomb of the Han dynasty. Look at it carefully and answer the following questions.

1 How many entrances do there appear to be to the farmhouse?

2 Why do you think there is such a high wall surrounding the farm yard and house?

3 What material do the Chinese appear to have used for the roof? Why might they have used this material?

SOURCE 7.4.1 Pottery model of a farmhouse of the Han dynasty

4 How many stories high is the building? Given this, what can you conclude about the level of Chinese technology when it comes to building?

5 Why might such a pottery object have been buried in a tomb?

WRITTEN SOURCES ABOUT SHI HUANGDI

Emperor Shi Huangdi of the Qin dynasty changed Chinese society greatly in his short reign. The lives of ordinary people were affected by his government's reforms. There is varying opinion, however, about whether these changes were good or bad for China.

Read the following two extracts carefully. They present different opinions about Shi Huangdi's reign. Then answer the questions that follow.

Your majesty rules a unified Empire in which the difference between right and wrong is as clear as your own total authority. Yet there are people who unofficially spread teachings that are against official orders … they openly criticise your comments … The people are thus encouraged to be disrespectful. If this lying is not stopped the imperial authority will be weak … all people owning books … should destroy them. Those who have not destroyed them within thirty days … are to be branded and sent to work as convicts.

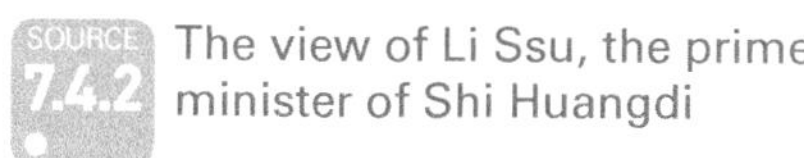
SOURCE 7.4.2 The view of Li Ssu, the prime minister of Shi Huangdi

The Qin rulers employ their people harshly, terrorise them with authority, embitter them with hardship, bribe them with rewards, and destroy them with punishments.

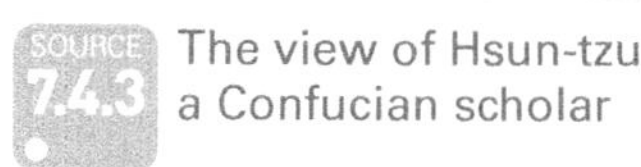
SOURCE 7.4.3 The view of Hsun-tzu, a Confucian scholar

6 Does Li Ssu's document support or criticise the Qin dynasty? Provide three examples that support your answer.

7 Why do you think Li Ssu ordered books to be destroyed?

8 What types of books would Li Ssu find especially threatening? Why?

9 Does Hsun-tzu support or criticise Emperor Shi Huangdi? Give three examples that support your answer.

10 How do you think Li Ssu would have responded to Hsun-tzu's writing? Why?

CHINESE PHILOSOPHIES

Philosophy is concerned with ideas and values. Philosophers attempt to explain humankind's place in the universe and consider how to create a good society.

In Ancient China during the Qin dynasty, there were three major and very different philosophies—Legalism, Confucianism and Daoism.

1 Opposite is a jumbled list of phrases that describe these three philosophies. Sort the list by copying each phrase under the correct heading in the table below. Conduct research on the internet or in your school library to help you.

Legalism	Confucianism	Daoism

- endorsed harsh punishments
- believed in the basic goodness of man
- based on scholarly teaching
- believed a happy life is brought about by understanding Dao
- endorsed harsh laws
- focused on social order
- disapproved of profit and personal gain
- outlined the code of Qin
- believed you should 'do unto others what you would have them do unto you'
- argued that everyone should obey the law
- believed that the fate of all things was influenced by understanding this philosophy
- endorsed strict laws
- believed peace was achieved through strong government
- focused on good government and a good society
- thought yin and yang were opposing life forces
- endorsed respecting parents
- believed government rights were greater than individual rights
- believed good behaviour towards others created a happy society
- believed that following the law was more important than having a good government
- sought order in family and in government

2 Complete the following paragraph about the three Chinese philosophies, selecting the correct words and phrases from the list below.

- laws
- Daoism
- Legalism
- peace
- philosophies
- history
- behaviour
- family

Confucianism, ______________________ and Daoism are the three most important ______________________ of Ancient China. Each was influential at different periods of ______________________ and each philosophy had a different emphasis. Legalism sought ______________________ and harmony with strong ______________________ and harsh punishments. By contrast, Confucianism stated that a better way of life was achieved by respectful and good ______________________ in the ______________________ and society. ______________________ put the responsibility for happiness and harmony on the individual.

7.6 CLIMB THE GREAT WALL OF CHINA

To climb some of the steps of the Great Wall of China you must answer the question on each step. Four possible answers are provided for each question. Highlight the correct answer. Start at the bottom and proceed to the next step as you correctly complete each question. Conduct research on the internet or in your school library to help you.

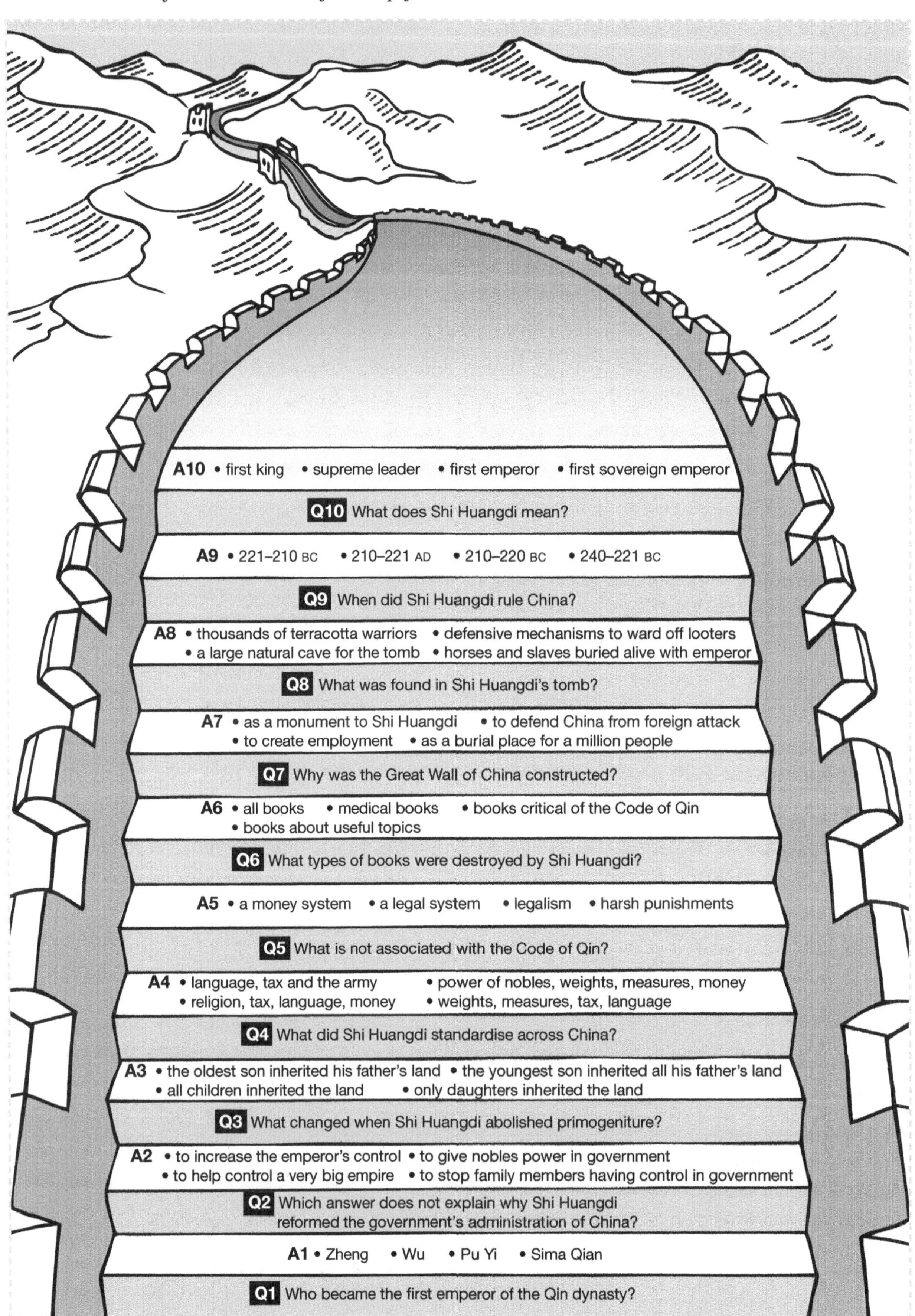

THE ODD ONE OUT

The Han dynasty was the last of the periods of Ancient Chinese history. The feudal system that had characterised the organisation of society made way for a system of government bureaucracy. Confucianism gained importance and China opened up a busy trade route with Europe along the Silk Road.

Below are descriptions of daily life during the Han dynasty. Find and circle the term that is the odd one out in each group. Conduct research on the internet or in your school library to help you.

1 Zhou dynasty / civil servant / important social class / government positions

2 examinations in the Five Classics / talent and ability / corruption / Han dynasty

3 second most important social class / wheat, rice, millet / traders / lightly taxed

4 craftsmen and women / processed raw materials / pottery, silk, porcelain / traders

5 well treated by government / merchants / lowest social class / motivated by profit

6 Wudi / 141–87 BC / Qin dynasty / emperor

7 Gongsun Hang / became emperor / swineherd / civil servant

8 mulberry trees / silk / cocoons / synthetic

9 craftsmen / traders / slaves / civil servants

10 civil servants / four social classes / emperor / farmers

11 tax revenue / Han Dynasty / small farmer land tax / no merchant tax

12 Chang'an / capital city / Shi Huangdi / Han Dynasty

13 grew farm produce / merchants / not respected / couldn't own land

14 300 000 students / 200 000 students / Imperial Academy / civil service

7.8 WHO AM I?

By the Han Dynasty in 202 BC to 220 AD, ancient Chinese society was organised into rigid social classes. The daily life of men and women varied depending on which class they belonged to.

1 Look carefully at the diagram of social classes in source 7.8.1 and conduct some research on the social classes of the Han dynasty on the internet or in your school library. Fill in the table on the following page to describe the social classes by writing a minimum of four dot points about each one.

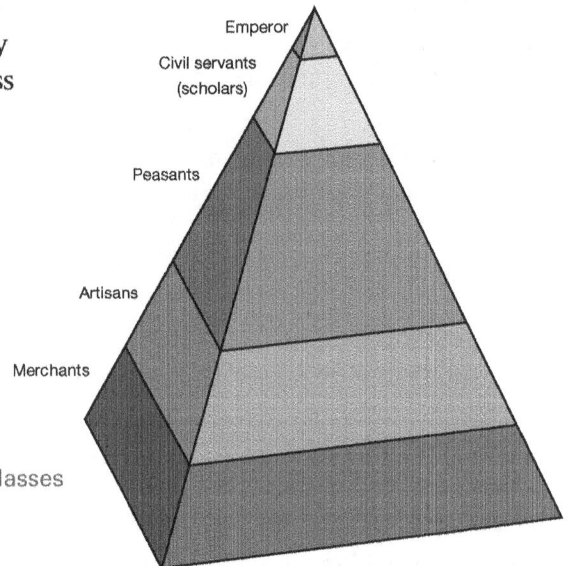

SOURCE 7.8.1 Diagram of the social classes in the Han Dynasty

2 After the emperor, which was the most important social class?

____

____

3 In Australian society today, business people are often highly respected. Why do you think they were the least important people in ancient China's Han Dynasty?

____

____

____

____

____

4 Why do you think farmers and merchants were taxed differently?

____

____

____

____

____

____

____

____

____

1 (continued) Social classes in the Han Dynasty

EMPEROR	
SCHOLARS/CIVIL SERVANTS	
PEASANTS	
ARTISANS	
MERCHANTS	

7.9 WORD SEARCH

Complete the word search related to the Shang and Zhou dynasties. The words to look for are listed below the puzzle.

T	C	H	D	K	B	R	O	N	Z	E	T	E	I	E	T	Y	O	T	I
P	X	E	M	K	Q	I	N	S	C	R	I	P	T	I	O	N	S	N	H
M	E	W	V	X	E	B	F	R	W	O	B	G	P	W	E	S	N	D	T
D	O	X	H	R	I	G	C	I	A	M	I	M	M	G	G	E	V	V	O
I	T	Q	Z	H	S	N	A	S	I	T	R	A	O	D	C	N	R	A	I
N	E	V	A	E	H	R	D	P	M	X	L	T	D	T	S	O	Y	M	B
R	F	O	R	T	U	N	E	T	E	L	L	I	N	G	T	B	H	T	D
K	T	A	L	T	C	A	F	E	T	R	A	N	O	H	O	E	I	W	X
R	Q	H	P	U	S	K	W	V	I	Z	A	K	T	J	I	L	M	S	N
P	K	I	B	H	G	N	A	Y	N	A	X	G	E	C	R	C	L	G	O
X	E	K	J	J	H	B	L	Q	C	O	F	N	L	M	A	A	U	N	I
F	R	Y	T	A	U	T	U	M	N	D	Y	I	E	A	H	R	O	I	T
Z	I	A	I	L	O	G	N	O	M	T	V	R	K	N	C	O	Y	K	A
U	P	Z	R	E	P	I	A	I	U	U	G	P	S	I	K	D	A	I	S
B	M	H	E	R	N	Q	D	C	A	A	K	S	J	H	P	R	N	Z	I
V	E	A	P	V	Q	S	E	T	A	D	N	A	M	C	V	O	G	D	L
E	W	A	R	F	A	R	E	F	W	K	E	J	M	H	X	W	N	K	I
S	T	F	H	M	O	P	U	V	M	C	K	Z	P	Y	Z	S	E	K	V
Q	D	A	Q	C	Y	G	E	U	G	P	C	R	O	S	S	B	O	W	I
G	L	A	D	U	E	F	X	V	B	H	H	H	N	U	E	I	U	U	C

Word bank

- Anyang
- army
- artefact
- artisans
- autumn
- bronze
- chariots
- China
- civilisation
- crossbow
- empire
- feudal
- fortune telling
- heaven
- inscriptions
- kings
- Luoyang
- mandate
- Mongolia
- oracle bones
- skeleton
- spring
- sword
- tomb
- warfare